CORPORATE CHICK TURNS INTO A SPIRITUAL HEALER

(Based on True Life Story)

Shweta Bisht

KALPAZ

ISBN : 978-94-5128-065-1

Price : ₹ 250/-

First Published 2014

Published by

Kalpaz Publications
C-30, Satyawati Nagar,
Delhi-110052
Ph. : 9212142040
E-mail: kalpaz@hotmail.com

Laser Typesetting : Shubham Printers, Delhi

Printed at : G. Print Process, Delhi

Cataloging in Publication Data—DK
Courtesy: D.K. Agencies (P) Ltd. <docinfo@dkagencies.com>

Bisht, Shweta.
Corporate chick turns into a spiritual healer : based on true life story / by Shweta Bisht.
p. cm.
Includes bibliographical references (p.).
ISBN 9789351280651

1. Bisht, Shweta. 2. Healers—India—Noida—Biography. 3. Spiritual healing—Hinduism. 4. Occultism. I. Title.

DDC 615.852092 23

PREFACE

I have kept the language of this book to be very simple and easy to understand for everyone. Even for common man who are not good in English language. Because I want this journey of my life or the truth of my life to reach to every individual who is seeking for help or is going through such type of problems. Hence, I have used simple English language here. May be grammatically in few places, I may not use appropriate syntax but please excuse me on that zone because this book is more than establishing myself as a "grammarian". I do hope this book will leave an indelible mark on everybody. My mission is to let this book be easily getting understood by all.

Kindly, excuse me for telling my emotions and feelings in such a way, if anyone read this book. I request him/her to forgive me for using these expressions for a moment and just imbibe the spirit and float into the truth of my true life experiences.

Hope everyone appreciates my feelings and contributions.....

Shweta Bisht

ACKNOWLEDGEMENTS

I am really grateful to all my Ex-Victims who motivated me to write this book. It was their belief and determination that inspiered me to narrate the hidden truths of the mysterious world, in which all of them were traped before.

A very special thanks to my mother "Sarojini Bisht", who stood by me in all my difficult times. And Above all, I devote this book to "Goddess Kali", as I have devoted my whole life to her...

STRAIGHT FROM THE HEART

Welcome to my world Friends......

This is a very emotional moment for me, because today I want to highlight every small things, happening of my life. Yes, sometimes peeping into your past can be very emotional and touching! You people may be thinking, why it is emotional? What's hidden in the shelves of the past? Well, I will surely reveal every bit of my truth of life in front of you people in detail. However, to pacify your hunger of curiosity, I would summarise my reason of being emotional with a short note : "My past consist of blend of emotions and experiences. Some were not expressable and some were full of helplessness and pain, few were filled with fear and not able to know that what was happening to me? Trust me, my friends, the feeling of helplessness and frustration in any form, crushes you from within.

Hence, I pray to *Maha Kali* to give me enough courage and the strength so that I could be able to reveal every bit of my life experiences with dignity, grace and humility. *Jai Maha Kali.....*

Yes, Maha Kali, She is the main guiding force for me, for whatever I am today. Her blessing helped me sail through all the hurdles of my life successfully. I will explain about her in detail to all of you. But before that I want to share something direct from my heart.

I have to admit gracefully that I was not very sure of writing this book. Nervousness and fear had crept into my psycho. In fact, I was in dilemma! How should I disclose things which are just hidden till now? And if yes then, how would the world accept it? Will they believe it? Will they laugh at it? Will they call me a psycho? Or will they simply ignore these facts? These were all the negative thoughts which have puzzled me.

Suddenly, a change takes place!! All the negative thoughts started fading away and I started feeling fresh, and positive which motivate me to write this book. A book that consists all my true experiences of life. My struggle, my courage, my fear, my never say die attitude, my faith, my transformation from a simple girl to a spiritual healer.

Another very strong reason of jotting down my feelings and true experiences was that people who are suffering from this problem, trying to explain about something unusual happening to their near and dear ones, who seek help, support, are mostly getting neglected and rather not taken by them seriously also. Those victims who are going through the zones of helplessness and frustrations internally can have a strong reasoning and show an article regarding this unknown world and unseen feelings that they are experiencing to their closed ones, and may be this sharing of my life true experiences helps them and their dear ones to atleast think once that yes what victim is saying can have some logical roots to it.......

May be my true story helps all those victims to prove

their trauma and pain to their known ones... So, I may extend my helping hand to all those people, who are facing these supernatural problems but people may not believe on them. Rest I want to leave it on god for helping and decide what future holds for my strong and emotional efforts... But I will be happy that I have done my bit honestly and tried to reveal the hidden truth of the unforseen things which cannot be seen with naked eyes to all the people but they do exist and they do make a damaging impact on the lives in a very strong manner.

Hence, the least that you can do is give respect to the supernatural things which may be out of your reach but that does not mean that they not true or they do not exists... Think about it with an open mind and heart for once atleast. May be you will be able to save yourself or your near and dear ones, who are trapped in these paranormal activities, but are unable to get out of these because people around them make fun of them, laugh at them, not believe them when they narrate their experiences and apprehension.

Every time thinking logically does not help. I am not saying about being superstitious but just open your eyes and spare a minute for things which are unknown to the common man, and yes supernatural power affects the common man very seriously when it attacks, and science has no solution for them.

Its True, science still hasn't got solution for many things. Science still has not reached to all the galaxies and planets or should I say all that exist around us. Science has its limitation too....

But one good thing has happend off late "Discovery Channel" and "History Channel" have started showing such type of things like "Most Haunted", "Paranormal Activities" etc, which are based on supernatural forces. So, if you guys and gals feel more confident on these shows then, I really don't mind you people believe on such supernatural activities through any medium ! Hence, there are still many things to get explored. The search is still on.... Its my request to all the readers here, that please do not be rigid about your perceptions regarding "Paranormal Activities" infact just open your eyes to analyse the new, not seen, not felt world around you. You can take it like studying or learning about a new subject which has been recently prescribed for your syllabus!!

Ok, so now I feel better, infact good after narrating my feelings with all of you readers. Hopefully, you will try to understand my feelings and emotions attached to this book now....

My Tribute To Goddess *Maa Kali*

So, lets start discussing the most important thing of my life! You must be wandering, what is it? Well its my kind, compassionate, and loving *"Goddess Kali"*. Yes, I dedicate this book to my *"Maa Kali"* and her love, blessings that she has showered on me till now, and I am sure She will continue to bless me like this till the end of my life... *Jai Maa Kali.*

Let me brief you about *"Maha Kali"* in my own little way. The way I see her, the way I feel her, the way I want people to know about her.

Yes, she is the Goddess of *Tantra.* Its very much true. But have you ever thought that is this the only identity that she has? Is this all that she is about? No, my friends, its not true. *Maa Kali* is not just the Goddess of *Tantra.* Infact today I want to clarify many myths about *"Maa Kali"*. Or should I say, that tell you more knowledge about her! Let me start from the very basic.

So, now I am going to mention the famous place for all devotees- *"Mata Vaishnav Devi" Dham.* Yes, when people are in pain, that visit this holy place every year or round the year for getting her blessings. Everybody knows about it in India and abroad. For my overseas victims, let me give you a brief about the holy place of *"Maa Vaishnav Devi"*.

It is a very sacred place where many devotees visit for their desires to be fulfilled. It is said that whatever you seek with honest heart will be answered with the blessings of the sacred spiritual powers. I hope that my overseas readers must have understood about the importance of visiting *"Maa Vaishnav Devi" Dham.*

So, now lets move forward with the point that I want to elaborate....

All of us visit *"Maa Vaishnav Devi"* for our own private personal desire as mentioned before too. Is not it? But now lets face it. How many of us actually knows about the fact that which are the goddesses present there? Do you know? If yes then very good. But if no, then let me make you aware about the fact that the goddesses present there are as followed:

1. *Maa Saraswati* – Goddess of Intelligence/art/communication

2. *Maa Lakshmi* – Goddess of money – who generates money

3. *Maa Kali* – Goddess who destroys human egoes.

Yes, my friends, the third goddess is *Maa Kali* who is present in *"Maa Vaishnav Devi" Dham*. People have this huge myth that the third goddess is "*Maa Durga*". For my overseas friends – "*Maa Durga*" is the name of another goddess in India. I want to keep my narration very simple to understand and not wanting to go into the vedic explanation and details of each goddesses at this juncture. Hence, will continue with the point of concern here....

My point here or my mission here is very straight. If "*Maa Kali*" is present in "*Maa Vaishnav devi*" *dham* and all the people visit there without any doubt or fear, then why don't I see people giving space to "*Maa Kali*" in their house temples? Why most of the people are scared of praying to "*Maa Kali*" in their house temples? When people can put a photo frame of "*Maa Vaishnav Devi*" in their house temples then why do they get scared of putting a photo of "*Maa Kali*" in their house temples? The reason is unawareness towards this. I have often seen people are suspicious if they see "*Maa Kali*", image in somebodyes house!! Maybe they think that the person who worships "*Maa Kali's*, image in the house temple is involved in some kind of "*Tantric* practises"!! Come on people, wake up!! wake up from this myths that have been practising since long from ages...

"*Maa Kali*" is considered to be the destroyer of human egoes, wrong ones, negativities around and taking care of her devotees like a mother. She is very kind and compassionate, loving goddess. She is always there to safegaurd her devotees in their difficult times. Yes, she is definately a fright to all dubion characters who have evil intentions. But she always answers her devotees in their distress.

Another wrong perception is that *Maa Kali's* puja can be performed only through sacrificing goat or other animals. But her puja can be done with *"Satvik way"* also. "*Satvik*" means pure – Anybody does not have to sacrifice any animal to please her. If someone worships her with rapt attention, that in though. Just pray to "Goddess *Kali*" with honesty and sincerety are sufficent. People think, if anybody offers costly things to *Maa Kali*, she will be pleased, Usually, greedy priests prescribe be such type of *pujas* for their own interest only to fulfill their own needs and selfish desire in the name of "*Maa Kali*". So beware of such wrong doers and misguiders in future now.

"*Maa Kali*" helps you for strong faith and honesty. A person who can protect himself/herself from this cruel world and can differentiate between the right and the wrong and must follow a correct path for himself/herself without any problem.

So, don't be scared to worship "*Maa Kali*" at all from now. We all need to be educated about the wrong notion. And the truth is that "*Maa Kali*" should be given a respectful space in your house temples without any fear. Worship "*Maa Kali*" with true heart and surrender yourself to her feet. "*Maa Kali*" will protect you, love you and taking care of you like your own mother.

Ok my readers all of this was possible through "awareness programme" you can pray to "*Maa Kali*" in the simplest form ever!!

Now, let me come back to myself and my life... I owe my life to "*Maa Kali*" completely, she is my real guiding force for whatever little I am today. She saves me, protects me, gives me the courage during the time when I GOT trapped in "Paranormal Activities". There was no one except her who saved me during that time. Hence, I feel happy to get so much of love from her. Thank you "*Maa Kali*" for your support, love and blessings. Just love me and protect me like this forever. *Jai Maa Kali....*

Sorry friends, sometimes I get carried away in the middle while talking about "*Maa Kali*" and her kindness. But what to do friends, I am her one of the true devotees and my life revolves around her only!! Hope you understand me.

"*Maa Kali*" now with your permission and courage that you have always granted me till now, I would like to start saying the truth of my journey. So "*Maa Kali*" give me all the courage to narrate it without any fear.

Jai Maa Kali.....

Remembering "*Maa Saraswati*", *Maa Lakshmi*, *Maa Kali*, I now start my true life story with.....*Om Shree Ganeshaye Namah* : –

Hey *Guys/Gals* you have entered the "world of truth" tie your seat belts fast and tight because it will be a roller-coaster ride for all of you now. Hope you enjoy and understand this journey!!

Sounded funny? Hilarious! full of carefree attitude? Fun loving? Adventurous? Like a teenager? Yes, I am sure it will make you feel that way Am I right? I know, I am!! This was the story of almost 16 years back. Yes, then my age was just 17. A complete innocent teenager, blunt, aggressive, full of fun, adventurous, all the time with friends, busy with extra -curricullar activities, being the class monitor, singing in the school choir, taking part in several competitions like – swimming (Butterfly stroke speciality), skating captain, wins several trophies and certificates for group singing competitions, taking part in creative writing, drama competition – I also took part in "Shankar's art competition" from school.

Hey, friends this reminds me of a very funny incidence during the competition. I want to share it with you now. The topic which was given to all of us was "Draw anything of your choice"!! Since I was very good in imitating any drawn picture, I started seeing around, there was nothing to imitate from then, I was in trouble? Suddenly, I saw a buffalo outside the lawn where all of us were sitting! And I started drawing that buffalo on my drawing sheet quickly and the only thing that I was praying every single second was that no one should drive away that buffalo. Otherwise, my drawing will be left incomplete!!! Well, at the end, I finally succeeded, as it was still there and I completed my drawing. I submitted my drawing sheet to the person concerned and started waiting for the result with eagerly...

Well the result was out. I, of course, did not win the competition but yes surely got a consolation prize and a certificate for drawing a good buffalo!! But still I was very happy!! And when I narrated this to my school friends later, they laughed their hearts out and even I laughed like a mad girl on this episode!! Oh god! those were the days...

Again I got carried away in the past and forgot to mention my school's name here!! Sorry readers, please excuse me this time. Let me introduce myself when I was studying in a school, and was a carefree teenager!

Ok, I was a student of DPS, Noida. I was very active in my school days and good in all subjects, except mathematics!! Oh god! I still remember that I used to hate maths period and always wanted to skip it!! Infact; mathematics was like one big horror for me in school and I just wanted to grow up quickly so that I could get rid of this subject once and for all!! Yes, I was thinking like that way.

And finally one fine day, that cherished moment came. I passed my 12th exam with flying colours. More than anything else we all was excited about not wearing the monotonous yet same old school uniforms at last! Now was the time for college life or college fun, I must say... But before I say anything about my further studies, there is one more thing that I would like to mention out here first.

Well, I would like to add here that I was very active and used to participate in every exhibition taking place in New Delhi, in between my summer and winter vacations. It was very good for me to earn pocket money and even spending it at my will!!

You guys/gals may be thinking that why I am telling this

episode in the middle of an uninterrupted story? So, my friends there was enough reason to tell this. This exposure with different clients, out of which mostly were "overseas clients" who came to India for exploring and expanding their businesses which gave me the confidence and vision of the corporate world. I started communicating with the Senior department heads of the multinational companies and from their my communication skills started taking a new leaf. It also gave me an opportunity to get practical knowledge about working in the corporate sectors, how do they carried out work smothly under pressure. At that time laptops were used by the selective business people only. And of course not like today's time, where every kid also has an I-pod and a laptop along with a Samsung galaxy or a Blackberry!! I thought that its better to present this infront of my young and teenage readers, or else they will think that what is wrong with Shweta Mam, why is she making such a big issue about a laptop.. After all its just a laptop buddy!! Hope you young readers have now got the point!

Yes, so coming back to my exposure from the exhibitions that I participated, gave me or rather started drilling the thought in me that I have to be liked by them. I have to be a leader, not a follower. For me seeing a manager of an multinational company handling his team members was a great source of motivation. I did smell the fragrance of authority and responsibility quite early, during my school days only which helped me to know about authority, leadership...., etc.

But then there was another thing that I really wanted to achieve! I wanted to clear civil service examinations. Infact, I always planned my subjects in school accordingly. And I knew that I could do this with my hardwork, persevenance and determination and prayed that my luck would or rather should work for me!!

Wait, I know what you people must be thinking about me as I was confused about my ambition? Sometimes, I talk about the corporate world and its exposure and my inclination towards it, and on the other hand, I just jump on to call civil services as my ambition. Wow! I am not sure about myself or what....

HMM.., no guys/gals I was not even a molecule bit confused. Infact, I was "street smart"!! Yes, I can explain this very well right now! Ok, lets start:

I said, that I wanted to be an "IAS officer" after clearing the civil service examinations, correct? And I called it my ambition also... Yes that was true. Hundred per cent true my friends. However, I knew many people who were preparing for civil service examinations and I used to speak to them often about their lectures and preparations. And most of them said that their Professors suggest them that its very good to have a thought of being an IAS/IPS/IFS officer, but not everyone could pass this examination and achieved the desired results. Hence, one must keep a back-up profession also, which helps them to stand up on their own feet with dignity, if unfortunately fate does not falls in their favour for this. Because otherwise they could get depressed. So one must take these examinations very seriously, however must not get trapped into the web of civil services only. Because life does not ends here. There are several other respected and dignified professions, too. And all the students studying for civil services should follow this tip or advice positively. See my friends, our job is to give our best in whatever we do, not necessary that by giving our best the tide will turn in our favour. But atleast we will have a consolation about the fact that we tried our level best and the rest we should leave it on to our fate and almighty.

So, I followed this advice very seriously and I want all my readers who are preparing themselves for any important examination, should all the time have a back-up plan or an alternative option to get success in life.

And I am sure that by now you must have understood as to why I called myself "Street Smart"! And your perception about me being confused about my ambition also would have changed by now completely!!

Yes, being a "corporate chick" was my second objective if "civil services" would not have worked for me....

Lets restart from the exposure that I experienced during the exhibition time. Trust me friends, this line of experience with overseas clients during that tender age really helped me a lot in later stage, which proved to be a blessing in disguise.

As mentioned earler that after the schooling usually got it was the time to decide for career. Everyone excited about getting admissions in the colleges. Cut out lists were out for several colleges.

I had focussed my attention for St Stephens only. I might get the admission through sports quota. One of my friends, who stayed in Noida near my house wanted to help me in this matter too, as she was applying for St Stephens too... she was very close to me, infact even today I remembered her. Though we are not in talking terms now, due to some misunderstandings, lets not get into such details here. Later, I will discuss the reason of our sour relations.

Anyway, I was in a fix. One hand, I wanted enjoy college life and get a good stamp on my educational qualification. And I was also planning to get admission into correspondence courses. And on the other hand, I wanted to start working as an intern in any of the good corporate companies for getting practical experience and of course not to forget that I had to create a back-up too as discussed earlier.

I took fifteen to twenty days to decide about my career's very important decision. And finally the decision came in the favour of joining a corporate sector for getting exposure, practical experience and earning some money for myself.

So, I joined correspondence courses in Political Science (Hns) in North campus. I got all the study materials, completed all the formalities. Now, was the time to search for a good corporate firm. But question was, which one? Where? How? When?

Meanwhile, when I was floating in my own delusion and opt for joining a good organisation. One of my friends just called me to say "hello" and that hello came at a very important time. He was my school friend, who was also searching for a job along with pursuing his career in correspondence courses!! And he informed me about a B.P.O... I did not know what a B.P.O. was all about at all!! He gave me an address in Gurgaon (adjacent to New Delhi). This important information is for my overseas friends you see... Oh! you guys/gals must be eager to know the name by now! The name of the organisation was "GE capital" The only one B.P.O. was present during that time in that region, with excellent reputation and known for its quality control. But as I mentioned earlier also, that I did not know what was it exactly and about what kind of work a B.P.O. does!! So very innocently, I asked my friend.. that please put some light into this matter. And guess, what the answer would have come from his side? Well, Shweta I also really didn't know what they do exactly, but the only thing that I knew was that they kept on picking telephone calls and talking to people in the night only... And for talking on the phone they were rewarded with good money my buddy!!! Isn't it a cushy job? He and I got very much excited and said, we are good in talking on the phone, so we would be absolutely perfect for this job!! So how to get this kind of job now? Moreover, we were more excited about stepping out of the house late night too!! We thought we could bunk the office one day and would go to any disco for clubbing also sometime in future...!! I am sure by now, you guys/gals must have had smiles on your faces after hearing this kiddish fact given here. But friends, I was talking about that time, when going out in the night with friends was not allowed or encouraged!! So, our "gang of friends" had to plan from very first day of the month how to arrange for this kind of night out. Even we planned what excuse to narrate in each other's houses for those outing. Anyway, so coming back to the target of getting the "Call Center" job...

So, now we had decided that I and my friend wanted this kind of job for sure. Reasons, I had already clarified in the last paragraph!!

While all this was going on in our minds, suddenly from some reliable sources, we got the news that there was a new Call Center opened in Noida, in the name of "EXL Services". This was U.S.-based Call Center, and had started hiring employees from G.E. Capital in bulk, because they had to start their "Pilot project" very soon. The new Call Center was also hiring youngsters for executive positions. Criterion is good communication skills, confidence, good english well-mannered and willing to work in the night shifs. So the interested candidates could either walk-in to the office premises or mail the C.V. in the given e-mail Id to the H.R. department.

YEPEE YEPEE YEPEE YEPEE...............

Well, this was my reaction after hearing this news and finally now I could go for the interview to the office address, specified by my friend.

I thought of going for the interview on the very same day, but then I had to wait for the next day to start because it was already eleven at the night by then.

The next morning, I got ready after wearing my fovourite T-shirt, blue jeans with my sport shoes and my hand bag and thought myself that I was looking good for this interview... with full confidence I reached the "EXL" office.

Oh my god!! what did I see? There was a long queue in the office for the interview and most of them were dressed in shirts and trousers, infact the girls even had make-up on.... There and then I felt like an idiot with my attire.. But still thought of hanging around there for giving the interview. No matter what may come.

Then my chance came, The persons who were coordinating the interview asked me for my C.V. But I didn't have my C.V., as I did not know what to write on C.V. being a fresher. She smilled back and said, take this blank paper and write your name, address, contact#, educational qualification, professional qualification on this; and give it to me. I followed her instructions and then she had send me for my first round of interview with the HR Executive.

The first question that was asked from me: Tell me about yourself. I said my name is Shweta Bisht, done my schooling from D.P.S. Noida. etc., in detail to the HR Executive.

The second question was about my hobbies? I said that I like swimming, talking to people, making new friends, etc.

The third question was that why do you want to join this Call Center? My answer was that because I like communicating with people over the phone and I like learning new things.

The HR executive smiles looking at my attire and said, I would send you for the second round, which would be with the Manager Operations. I really didn't understand what this position meant at all. But still I said ok confidently and went to another cabin where the "Manager Operations" was sitting with his laptop on... Even he asked me the same questions and then he asked me a very important question at last! What is your expectation? I said Rs. 10,000, instantly. He looked at me with surprise and said, you are a fresher and the salary slab for this executive position is Rs. 8,000 not more than this. Then why should we pay you Rs. 10,000? I really didn't know what happened to me my friends and I answered his question very politely and confidently in the following way:–

Yes, I agree that I was a fresher in the Call Center area. However I was not a fresher completely in the field of communication. I had worked in the exhibitions held at Pragati Maidan with multinational companies; dealt with their clients, giving them the specified information, convinced them for certain policies and benefits regarding the company and persuaded few important clients for them as well. I had good experience in handling the overseas customers which I did with confidence and able to understand their accent and language without any problem. Hence, I had gone through some practical knowledge which proved that I was not a fresher in the field of communication. So I felt that I deserve to be given the Rs.10,000 per month slab as my salary. Otherwise, I would not be comfortable.

The moment I completed my last word, the Manager of Operations smiled, looking at me and said Ok Shweta, approving Rs.10,000 per month as your gross salary, your take home salary would be Rs. 8,500 per month, hope now this will make you happy.

I had a glint in my eyes after hearing this from him and I said, sure it would, thank you. He told me to go for my last round of interview with the H.R. Head. So, I went there next. There she just read something written on my CV and started explaining me my salary break-up like this way:–

- Rs.10,000 is your gross salary (per month).
- Rs. 8,500 per month would be your take home salary.
- You would get free One meal served by us.
- Cab pick you up from your house and even drop you back.
- There would be night shift.
- Your date of joining would be from next month.

So, did you agree with all these formalities and conditions? I said: Yes, I agreed.

Then she handed over a LOI (letter of intend) to me with my date of joining specified on it, alongwith my designation of "Customer Care Executive" for U.S.-based process on it. Said, congratulations to me and I said thank you to her in return and came back home happily.

My mother was very DELIGHTED to see my LOI with Rs.10,000 as my monthly salary and knowing that a good company had choosen me to be a part of their team.

I started waiting for the next month eagerly, so that I could attend my first day in office and got to know what exactly happened there....

Finally, that day came. I was really excited. At 4.30 evening the cab came at my doorstep and I see youngster like me sitting in it. It was Tata Sumu! I sat in it said Hi, to everyone and reached office happily. We had to wait in the cafeteria area, which was very well-funished and good with a television also. All of us were really suprised seeing that an office kept TV for us!! Then our names were called out and a group of 45 people were formed to enter the training room nearby.

Finally, after a long wait all of us entered the beautiful training room, with a projector, creatively organised seating arrangement for the candidates. Then came the HR executive for "Induction", telling us or shall I say, briefing us about the company's profile and its departments and nature of work, etc. Then she gave us different kinds of forms to fill, along with taxation form, etc. Basically, first day was only for completing the Induction.

Later, we were informed that its the dinner time and the food was ready in the cafeteria area. So, we went there to have food. It was a good . We enjoyed it, and then again went back to our training room. Then came the time of introducing each other and knowing about each other more closely and different games were also played. First day was a complete chilled out day and then the shift got over and we headed to our respective cabs and finally I came back home, early morning. I changed my clothes and went off to sleep. Then got up in the afternoon for lunch. Ate my lunch and then started getting ready for my office once again. The cab came on time, I sat inside it, reached office.

Today, was the day of meeting our trainer. To be more specific our "Voice and Accent trainer", who would teach us how to understand the "neutral accent", and help us to get rid of "regional accent", if any... Make us aware about the cultural differences and thoughts of Indians and the US people. Enhance our communication skills, make our speech more refined and also very importantly how to slow down our "rate of speech". Infact much more than what I had specified which to be done....

So, the trainer walks-in with positive body language and a big smile on his face. He introduced himself us and narrated about his work experience and all the above that I mentioned to you a minute before. The whole day went in this way and finally the night ended and we headed back to our cabs and then I reached home. Slept immediately.

The next day, when I reached office we were given "ID cards" or the "Access cards" that we had to touch on the "access machine" fixed at every floor of the office, the moment we entered the office. This would keep a record of our attendence and even our break times and login and logout times too!! Hearing this all of us were excited and really liked this new concept. So, we wore the access card on our neck like a necklace. Our voice and accent training went on till 15 days. Then was a written exam and an oral exam, which had to certify to go to the next level. That was "Process Training", in which an another trainer would teach us about the "Process" or the work that we needed to do. Results came out I was certified as the first level of "voice and accent" training was successfull. Then, the certified group was sent for the process training.

The "Process training" was for a month. I was in the "U.S. process" of "House Mortgage", in the name of "Mobile Housing Division", and we were to take care of its customer service department. It was a tough process training, but at the end of it, I did that also quite well with case.

Now, was the time to hit the floor. Meaning going and starting the work on our specified work stations. I was in the "Pilot process batch". But before that we were sent to the floor for listening to the calls (live calls) of our senior executives. It was called "Call bargins", in which we had to be quite and only listen actively for gaining experience. This was for 15 days. After that we would be independently handling the calls by ourselves.

Finally that day came, when I had take my first call. We were distributed in different teams with our Team leaders. My first call was with an old lady, and she wanted to know her due date of the payment, alongwith the due amount in total. See, I still remembered it after so many years!! I successfully gave her this information by going to the right screen of my computer and I was very happy about it. Slowly, the days started running with high pace of work and learning experiences. With each new call and each new problem solving techniques or rebuttals. I became confident about my work and started understanding the Call Center designations, its authority and its exposure too. Six months passed after. I achieved a good spending power too. I had my own zero balance, corporate account in which every month without any fail the salary used to get transferred automatically. My work life was rocking and my studies were also going on during the two days off that I used to get.

One fine day, I was sitting on my work station and that day the call flow was not very heavy, so I didn't have much to do. So I was just looking around from my work station around the floor area. Suddenly, my eyes caught the attention of a higher level constructed stage, that belonged to all the team leaders of that particular floor. That was the area from where they used to keep an eye on all of their team members.

Of course, I had seen that area and my team leader before, but just because I used to be very busy taking calls successfully, never saw that area and its authority with this kind of vision. The vision was to be there now. I also wanted to be a team leader now. I wanted to grow now. I wanted a higher designation than an executive. The next level was of a senior executive and then came the team leader. I now wanted to be a team leader for sure. Day and night I started thinking how can I make this possible? How? I started sitting with my senior customer care executive and supervisors for understanding their nature of work. The new exposure that I got here was that they were the ones who would handle much more difficult calls than a normal customer care executive, handle customer who are badly irritated and frustrated with some bad service provided to them. For achieving this level, I had to concentrate more on my rebuttals and had to have the skill to solve these complicated or escalated calls. I opened up my process training manual once again back home and started studying the sensitive details and minute details given in it too. Slowly and slowly I started applying it on my calls and the results started coming out to be more positive. I even started helping my team members once caught in the problem while having an irritated customer. I started coming to the notice of my team leader. She called me and said that I could try taking supervisors calls now, if any help would be needed then she is there for me. I was very happy and I started taking and solving escalated calls for my team now. By then nine months passed. My hunger for being a team leader started getting increased. But there was stagnation in my team. I decided to change my organisation now. Look for an organisation where I get hired as an team leader directly.

I got myself registered with few consultants now. Seeing a good brand like EXL services and my work experience, they started offering me many jobs. But my criteria was of being a team leader.

Then one day I got a call from a company's HR executive, offering me a position of senior executive in an out found process of US, sales process in which we had to sale telecom connections of sprint PCS, MCI, etc. And if I would exceed my sales target mentioned, for three month then. I would be promoted to a "team leader" in three months from the joining day and of course with higher salary than my present company was offered too. This offer sounded really interesting to me and I thought of grabbing it.

I went for the interview and I got selected. I had to join after one month. I gave one month notice to my present company and after one month, I joined "Flex Contact Center" as a senior customer care executive. Now, again this was a night shift style of working being a U.S.-based process. And this time the target was to achieve the position of a "team leader". Finally, the day arrived of joining the new Contact Center and the first day of work was again Induction, introduction, form filling etc. This time the Voice and Accent trainer was an"American trainer", who flew from America to teach us different things. This was a new exposure to all of us again. Since it was a outfound process, it had more high energy level with it on the floor. Sales targets, performances, team sales scores, etc. We started selling the cell phones one by one. Understood the sales techniques, USPs, etc., in the process. I learned the difference between customer service zone and sales zone. As the focus was only on the target to be achieved, I started doing good amount of sales regularly and in three months I was then promoted to a "team leader". I was really very happy and feel that finally today I achieved my desired target. I was assigned a team of 25 team members. I was given a worshop of leadership, quality, team-management after this. I got really busy with all of this. Then I was taught how to distribute call flows, was introduced to different kinds of "diallers" available, call filterations, etc. It was a very good learning process for me. This was how my professional life was on its great going....

Let's talk a little about my personal life also! I realised that the plans and the dreams that I and my friend had made together, remembered, going to the club, night life, bunking office, etc., were just sleeping under the graveyard shift (night shift). I felt that how kiddish we were, we did not have any time for socialising now!! But this, didn't effect my desire of achieving great height in my career at all. It was just a passing thought that came to my mind all of a sudden.

Hey, did I tell you people, about my loveable pet dog "Jimmi", a pomorarian breed, white in colour, male by gender. He came into my life when I was in first standard. I used to really love him a lot. He was one of my best friends ever. He used to sit with me while I used to complete my home-work, watching TV, play with me, I used to take him for evening walks too. I had my best times with him. I loved Jimmi, I missed my pet still. The reason I mentioned "Jimmi" here because when I joined for work, he had gone old, he started getting weak also. But was still healthy. Dogs are a very important factor in every human-beings's life. One day, Jimmi died, because of his age getting over as per his breed. He lived for 14 long years with us. We buried him nicely with lots of love and care and I still remember that it was the month of May, when he died. I felt very lonely after that, but tried to divert my attention to my work. After that I never thought of keeping a dog realising that it gives immense pain to you when he is no more. But Jimmi taught me to understand the body language, expression, movements of dogs, understanding the animals gesture very well. Where all of this helped me, soon I would reveal it to you, people.

Life was going on with full swing, Salary, independence and dignity. Suddenly, one day something strange happend.... As usual I was getting ready to tell my team that soon it would be the logout time, swiftly close some more sales before the day got over.

I yelled and finally said LOG OUT GUYS.....

The moment I completed saying this statement I felt someone was standing behind me. I thought some team leader would have come to my work-station to inform about something. So, I immediately turned my neck back to see who it was. But there was nobody!! I felt surprised!! But never took it seriously, thinking that it would have been an illusion.... So, I came back home and slept nicely. Then as per my daily time-table, I got up, had my lunch and started getting ready for my shift once again... I went infront of the mirror for combing my hair. I had very long hair, till my waist, infact I still have fortunately!! While I was combing my hair I felt that again someone is standing behind me, but this time the existence was felt more strongly than before, so I again turned back to see, who it was... But again there was no one at all!!!

And this time I felt a little weird, because it was only me in my room and I was absolutely fresh after I got up from a nice sleep.

Meanwhile, my cab arrived and I started walking towards it, thinking about what I just felt! It was the second time, that this happened...

Hey, has anything like this happened with anyone of you who is reading this book? If no, then it is very good, but it YES, then, do think about it seriously, atleast try to know why? Precaution is better than cure. Because I wish I would have done this at the very first time when I felt weird.....

Anyway, no one could turn back time...

Yes, you are right friends "Black Magic" in my life had arrived with its first step towards me. From here you would read the slow poison effect of black magic and how it could destroy someone's life totally without any one knowing about it!!

Now, I would introduce you to another hidden aspect of my life, or should I say, a chapter that I didn't elaborate till now. Question arises why? Why I did not mention it till now while I was narrating about myself? Yet? What is in store now? The answer to all these doubts and questions is that its very difficult for me to once again go back to those memory lanes, which I blocked forever. But since this book is about true life experience, I had to walk back into those memory lanes for sure... Hopefully, you people would walk with me on them as well by feeling and understanding each and every line or statement that I mentioned here from heart...

I belong to a Rajput family. As, I mentioned earlier about my nature and being a tom-boy at the same time, I had boys to be my friends, more than girls.

I also mentioned about me, participating in the international exhibitions at Pragati Maidan, that gave me an excellent exposure in work field. Hope you guys/gals remembered it! One thing that did not mention during that time was about a guy whom I met there. One day, I missed my bus and hence he helped me to reach back my home by the staff bus available from Pragati Maidan. Our first meeting was not very favourable. I thought of him to be over-smart, flirtish by nature. However, I just wanted to reach back home safely, hence I did not aswered back that day!! Next day, I got my friend introduced to him. Names and identity of each member that I am mentioning here will be kept confidential because I really don't believe in harassing or degrading any one.

In short, we all became friends and had a group of people who used to participate in these exhibitions whenever possible. Meanwhile, he started liking me and one fine day proposed me for being his girl friend. I said no due to my personal reasons and different religions that we belonged to. I am not against any religion at all but that time I was not prepared for this courageous and revolting step at all!! He felt sad. But again he tried to convince me, again I refused. This happend five times, but I didn't agree at all. I yelled badly at him this time infront of his friends in frustration. He walked away slowly.

Then one day suddenly, he proposed me as usual after some days went by. This time his eyes were red and his body language was ~~also a~~ bit strange. Slow, eyes focussed on me. Strangely, this time when I looked towards him to once again say no to him, I got glued to his eyes and was unable to look anywhere except his eyes, which were red and not blinking. And I said yes, I am ready to be your girl friend..... He smilled and we walked together, he dropped me back home and the only thing that I had in mind was this guy!!

This time I wanted to ask all of you that what do you think this was? True love from myside or something forcefully done? Why and how once I said yes to this guy after refusing so many times? Some may say that may be my heart would have melted for him at last/ some may say that the guy's true love for me finally made me say yes to him! Some may also think that we were made for each other!! Right! But, can it be anything more serious than this bollywood effect? You must think about it my readers. Remember that each and every word that I am specifying here is true and not a gimmic or self-made fake item story. It is the truth of my life, hence respect it and try to understand it with clean heart.

Ok moving on to the same point, have you seen anyone in your contact changing or accepting something all of a sudden, for which he/she was totally against? Or has this sort of thing happened with you ever? If yes, then this coming up information is only for you!!

The sudden change in my behaviour was due to the influence of "supernatural process" called *"Vashikaran"* or "Forcefully attracting someone towards you". It's not hypnotism but yes very much like hypnotism. I would talk about it in detail later.

There was nobody to tell me about this at that very time or help me because I was completely unaware of this process existing, being a normal girl. But today I want you people to be alert about such changeable behaviour caused on your near and dear ones. If anything so unexpected happens with you or any one that you know then don't wait and just consult a "Paranormal Expert" or a "spiritual healer" quickly. Before it gets too late... why I am saying this? Because it got very late for me. How? Listen carefully, I started following this guys instructions blindly, whatever he used to say, was like Bible for me!! Yes readers, I am not exaggerating it, its true. I am a one example of this deadly process affecting my life. How? I mentioned about changing my job from EXL Services to Flex Contact Centers, right. One thing I did not mention earlier that I faught with my house holder and took a separate rented house and started staying there alone, as they were not agree to accept my relationship with this guy! Yes, I did this too... This was one of my biggest blunders of my life. My parents tried to make me understand that what I was doing was completely wrong, and this guy is not worth for me. But I was completely trapped in this "Black Magic-*Vashikaran*" process done by him on me. This was revealed to my family by one of my families' guruji that I would talk about him later. So, now do you agree that how deadly and dangerous this process could be for your children, husband, wife, yoursself, if anyone of them is trapped in it, that particular person becomes like a puppet in the hands of the person who has applied this on him/her!!

One more thing that my lovely dog Jimmi died in the month of May as I said before also, and I left my house just within six months from that particular month!! Have you ever heard that dogs take over negativities on themselves, especially if there is anything supernatural involved? They can also sense and feel spirits around!! Yes my readers, its true. So if you see your dog barking or crying out of the blue, looking at something or looking around, then don't think that he/she has lost it! May be there is something out there that you are unable to see or feel, but this lovely faithful creature is trying to save you from it or alerting you from its negativity....

Then he left for Saudi Arabia regarding a job contract of eighteen months. I was back in India only, waiting for him to meet again! For these eighteen months I did not go to any movie hall, did not meet my friends, did not go for any parties, nothing I did without him!! Yes guys, nothing at all. Eighteen months no recreation at all, is not normal at all! Only used to speak with this guy over the phone, when he used to call me. Write long letter to him, about what all I did here in a week, meaning I used to write him every week!! completely weired....

Is anything like this happened with anyone that you know? If yes then you know what to do now!! Consult an expert regarding this abnormal behaviour. Please do not go to a psychiatrist, go to a "paranormal expert" and a "spiritual healer", for guidance. Someone who is genuine and not fake.

Ok everybody, now lets return to my office day senario that I mentioned. Forgot? Let me remind you once again. Remember, we talked about me combing my hair and looking in the mirror, I felt someone was standing behind me for the second time, but when I turned back there was no one. This made me think for little longer this time that what this could be? My cab arrived and I sat in it and started thinking on this continuously. Hope you remember now, that where we left the story.... Lets continue further...

So then I finally reached the office, but this time I was a little lost at the same time in my thoughts about the mirror episode, along with it I kept on doing my work. But that day I could not completly concentrate on my work. The day ended and I came back home and slept again. When I reached home, it means the house that I had taken separately from my parents' house after fighting with them over this guy!! I was staying absolutely alone out there. Then around 5'O clock in the evening I woke up, but still was lying down on the bed with my face looking upwards to the ceilling area, where the fan was moving in high speed. I thought now I should get out of bed and get ready. The moment I moved my leg a bit to get up....

Wait guys/gals let me just have a deep breath before narrating this episode because you to as it still gives me shivers down to my spine when I think about it... I felt two hands pressing my neck and vocal chords with immense force. Someone was trying to kill me but I could not see anyone, no hands were visible, no one was visible, the only thing that was there, were the strong gripof two hands throttling me badly. I felt as if today was my last day of life, infact last moment of few breaths were left. I was scared to the core. My room light's were off, hence there was complete darkness. Then I touched my neck with my both hands, and could feel strongly that it was somebody's hands, two hands, pressing my vocal chords with lot of force. I got more scared. I gave up all hopes, this time, after feeling those hands, with my own hands. Suddenly, something strange happened..... I remembered the mythological serial based on *Maa Kali*, the way she was destroying all evil forces and demons with her weapons... And I still don't know that from where I spoke with lot of struggle – *"Maa Shakti"* (*Maa* give me the power) and imagined her image in my mind and heart. The moment I said this, those two hands left my neck immediately and I got out of bed and switched on the room light. The very same moment I felt that something travelled out of my room window as fast as light!! That was it...

I ran out of that house which was located on the second floor of a building with open doors, without realising that some thief could have entered seeing the main entry door being kept completely opened! But when you feel or experience anything 'supernatural' then nothing else stays in your mind. I mean no logic, no sense works that time. So, then I rolled over on the stairs, again got up, lost all my senses for that very moment and just ran on the road with terror and fright around me. Guys/gals, I still have wound marks on my feet and elbows present, which I got while falling from those stairs in haste with fear!!

I just ran and ran... people were staring at me that what went wrong? I reached a P.C.O. I thought of calling this guy for whom I had separated from my parents. I picked up the receiver of the landline phone to dial the phone number, but I didn't know what to dial?? Yes, I had forgotten all numbers that time due to fear and terror of what just happened!! The P.C.O. shop guy was looking at me with strange looks as to what Am I upto? What was wrong? He asked me, is everything Ok? I looked at him with helpless eyes, I was crying with fright, my face was red, my hair were all tangled up, why slippers were not there, I had to run bare foot, my clothes were dirty as I was falling and rolling on the stairs, basically I was looking completely lost mentally. I was not getting the words as to what should I tell him, my voice was choked as it failed to spell a single word. He gave me a glass of water quickly and told me to sit there on the chair and relax. He also told me to take some deep breaths for cooling me down. While I was following his instruction, I saw my common friend. I said common friend because he was a common friend between me and that guy for whom I had left my house. As I said that I would keep the names confidential in this whole journey. So I shouted by his name and he came towards me with surprise. He was taking his dog for an evening walk. His dog's name was "Sky".

The moment I saw his dog I asked him, do you have *"Hanuman Chalisa"* at home? Before he could ask me anything about my appearance and status, I again repeated the same question to him, this time with little irritation. He instantly said "Yes, I do have", but what happened? I was in complete panic situation. I said, then go and get it immediately and come to my house with your dog urgently, I am waiting downstairs for you. He just could not make out the head or the tail of what I was saying, and why! He gave an extremely confused look at me but did go to get the things that I told him. Within 15 minutes he got what I said and I was waiting for him downstairs of my house which was on the second floor. I took the *"Hanumanji's Chalisa"* from him and pressed it in my hands lightly remembering Hanumanji with pure heart asked him for courage so that I could climb the stairs of my house where I just experienced such a horrific moment some times back.... We started climbing the stairs slowly and finally reached at the main entry door of my house which was kept still opened. I instructed my friend that listen – "There is something that just happened to me few minutes back, which I would narrate you after a while but before that I wanted to make myself sure about what I was thinking and what I experienced!

He again gave me a strange look. But agreed, he was quite. I then said we would enter the house with your dog along, wherever I would point out and say that see there was something out here, then I wanted to see whether your dog was able to sense it or not! Because I heard that dogs could sense supernatural things around... He was shocked hearing this, felt weird, but was quite again. Finally, we entered the house. First came the drawing room or the sitting room, I felt nothing abnormal there, dog was also cool about that room. Then we went to the kitchen, all clear there too checked the washroom, everything was fine there too! Stepped in to the guest room, I and the dog were Ok there also!

Finally, one room was left, the same room where I experienced the attack, while running away with fright. I had banged the door of the room and it was closed. I said to my friend that listen, I would open this door and if I feel something abnormal then point out at that angle immediately and I want to see if your dog feels the same or not we were ready for this now. So, when I opened the door, I felt something was sitting on my mattress area and I was about to point my finger towards it, but before I could do that, the dog jumped at once on to the mattress and started barking loud looking at that particular angle, and then changed his position after few seconds and jumped towards the right side of the floor and barked towards the window, situated in that room. And trust me guys/gals that I felt each and every moment of the unknown thing around in that room followed by that dog. Then all of a sudden he stopped barking and became quite. Now, I realised that the 'supernatural thing' was no more there!!

My friend was shocked standing there. I sat down being blank on the same mattress along with "Sky", the dog and patted him on his back. Saying thank you my dear for helping me to be make sure about my feeling.... Now my friend had several questions ready. I looked at him with surety in my eyes this time. Even I was ready to narrate him about the whole incidence which left me in daze. I told him each and every little thing that happened and he was surprised and said to me – "what the hell is going on"? My friend and I were sitting together for whole one hour and then I asked him, do you want to have tea? He said, yes I made two cups of tea and gave "Sky" few biscuits and sat there to discuss the happenings and what he had seen with his own eyes too. He said to me listen – This is very scary to hear and believe.... Then he called that guy... Hey, I am tired of calling him "That guy", "That guy". Why don't we all give him some name here? Just a hypnotical name!! So what it should be? Hmm.... How about "Mr Dash"? Yes! Lets call him "Mr Dash". Dash— because in the dash space one could fill anything. So, I gave you guys the liberty to call him by any name after you read the whole book. You could call him

Mr Dash or "Mr whatever", after analysing the whole story!! Ok, so its decided that we would refer to him as "Mr Dash" from now in this book. Lets continue....

My friend called Mr Dash and told him to come immediately to my place without wasting any time. He asked my friend what happened? My friend said that just come here and then we would tell you everything here only. Mr Dash asked that Shweta is back home right now? Hasn't she gone for her shift tonight? My friend answered – No its all about her and she is very much present here, we are waiting for you to be here urgently. Mr Dash could not understand anything and came to my house immediately. He reached by no time looked at me and asked "Why are you looking so tensed and scared"? My friend and I looked at each other and narrated everything to him innocently. He heard everything patiently and then at last said – How could all this be possible? No, I don't believe this. This cannot be true. The moment he said this, my friend shouted back at him saying – what do you mean how its possible? Its the fact. I have seen all this abnormal activity happening with my own eyes. I was the witness to it. I told him to calm down. I told "Mr Dash", that see, this is exactly what happened, and there be no eif and but' about it. Its the truth, now tell me what should be done. Because I could not stay here after experiencing such a hair-raising episode. My friend also agreed to it. That night no one slept. Three of us were kept awake. Mr Dash prepared food with my friend. Made me eat the food and then discussed about this episode again.

Finally, we decided that may be there is something wrong with this house and we should think of shifting from here as soon as possible. Then it was 6'O clock in the morning and now I was feeling sleepy. I wanted to sleep, but I was scared, too. But, both these guys told me that its morning time now, and nothing wrong could happen. I agreed and hence went off to sleep in the guest room this time, with *Hanumanji's Chalisa* with me.

Meanwhile, these two guys went back to their home saying, that they would come back here during the lunch time with food to eat for me. I agreed. They came back around 2'O clock in the afternoon. I was still sleeping. Mr Dash had the extra keys for my house, based on trust I gave it to him. They woke me up. We ate food together and then they suggested me to go to the office that day, so that I feel a bit distracted from last night's episode. I also felt that yes that would be good for me. So, I started getting ready for my office. My cab arrived and I went to my office, totally blank, lost, in a nervous state of mind. The only thing that was going on in my mind was that I had to shift from that particular house on an urgent basis. I couldn't concentrate in work for the first time!! I was tensed about my shifting and this strange problem that I had experienced 24 hours back.

The biggest hurdle for me was that I could not even tell this to anyone in my office, because they would not believe it or either make a fun of me. I wanted my shift to get over quickly for the first time and I should go back and make calls to property dealers for finding a new house for me.

And the wait got over, my shift ended. I came back home. Suddenly, there was a door bell ringing at 9'O clock morning. I opened the door. I saw my neighbours on the door, I said hello to them and invited them inside my house. There was an aunty and his son who came to meet me. I asked them what happened? Why are you looking so surprised? Very hesitantly aunty holding my hands with both her hands and asked me – "Is everything Ok my child"? I didn't understand why she is asking me this question? I asked her what happened aunty, are you trying to tell me or inform me about something? She was quite and gave me an expression of an "yes".

Finally, she told me that my child I want to ask you something. May I? I said, of course aunty please ask me without any tension or stress. She said the most weird thing to me! I could not believe my ears for few seconds. She said "my dear child we had seen you climbing up the stairs towards the terrace area after 1.30 in the night, fews times after you have shifted here and standing on the terrace alone for hours, not talking to anyone, no cell phone and looking down from the terrace wall, as if you were searching for someone, standing down. Once my son went up on the terrace for a smoke late night around 1.30, and he saw you standing there alone. He also called your name, to ask you that why you were standing alone at such late hours. But you never turned back to answer him. This was very strange to him. He came downstairs that night and told me everything. Then he started keeping an eye on you after this strange behaviour! And kept on checking the terrace during late night hours, if you were again present there alone. And more than twice more he found you standing the same way and not responding even after calling your name!! He found this very surprising and spooky"!!

Hence, we decided to come and talk to you today! What is going on? Is everything Ok dear? Do you need any kind of help? Please tell us, we are there. Hope you are not thinking of committing a suicide my dear child!! I then opened my mouth to say – Aunty just a minute please. I am not understanding anything that you just told me!! They were shocked and asked me – what do you mean? I said aunty, I had never ever gone upstairs in the night alone, why should I go there? As usual, I was at my Call Center office and I left my place at 5.30 maximum in the evening!! I was not even there. Don't you see the lock on my entry door? She said we did, but we thought that you locked your house to go to the terrace!! I said – aunty it was not possible. Its, definitely not me, your son must had seen someone else in upstairs. The moment I said this, the son sitting there, just interuppted me suddenly – No it was you, I am sure, don't make me a lier, we were worried for you, so thought of coming and talking about this to you. We never came here for getting insulted and being called as liers.... I said calm down please, I am not saying anything like this to you. Its just, that I never go to terrace in the night, I am serious about this. Suddenly, all of us became quite. Then three of us said one think together – " Then who was she"? Again we looked at each other with surprising expressions and this time with lot many questions also!! Aunty says – "My child there is something really wrong then". From the time you have shifted here, we have noticed that the street dogs have started crying and howling from 2 to 2.30 in the night regularly!! I looked at her and said – what do you mean by this aunty? Are you trying to say that I am evil? or unlucky? She immediately answered back saying - "no, no, not at all my dear, I am just trying to match the missing links and happening with the time duration that it has started happening. Please don't take me otherwise...." I said Ok, fine aunty. I offered them a cup of tea and then we started the discussion on a more serious front.

I confessed to them that yes, strange things have started happening with me from the time I have shifted here... I narrated, all the earlier happening stories to them in length. And I also said that I think there is something wrong with this house I guess! Hence, I am planning to shift immediately from this house now. They were shocked hearing my side of the story, and aunty said that my child there is something very seriously wrong with this place and you also seem to be in some big problem that we are unable to gaze right now. Then suddenly she asked me – my dear where is your "house temple"? In India mostly in all houses we have a small place for praying and worshipping, where we also keep idols of gods or goddesses too, according to our religion and belief. This is called "house temple". This definition is for all my overseas readers. Lets continue... So she asked me this question. I said sorry aunty I haven't yet made that place for "house temple", I didn't have a "house temple" in this house. Hearing this she was shocked and said that – How could you do this my dear? You must have a "house temple", immediately here. Do this today only. It is very important. If there is anything negative, it will become weak once you start praying in your "house temple". I said Ok aunty, I will do this. She told me if anything happens where I need her help then I should not feel hesitant at all for approaching her. I thanked her for her concern and they went back to their house.

Before I proceed further, let me ask my readers guys/gals one question. Has anybody told you or have you ever heard or felt that there is someone like you, who is seen in the night walking alone or standing alone in dark and never turns around when called? If no then very good, you are safe. But, if yes, then it is alarming for you my dear. Don't neglect this sign at all!! It can turn out to be very dangerous in the near future! How? Why? You will read now and understand.

So, then after when both aunty and her son left, I started thinking of shifting from this place more urgently. I was scared and at the same time curious also, about who was standing there on the terrace, who was misunderstood with my identity and looks? Many questions were roaming in my head. And yes, even the street dogs did cried and barked in the night from 2 to 2.30 for 5-10 minutes, I noticed it whenever I had an off from the office. Have you heared dogs crying or howling in the middle of the night consecutively? If yes then may be they are seeing some evil spirit or practise infront of them, which we are unable to see!!

Oh, I remembered that aunty advised me to make a "house temple" immediately. I started walking towards the market area to get my things for "house temple" and I was very much eager to make it too!! Finally, I reached the shop from where one could get all the "worshipping stuff". I entered the shop and the moment I wanted to call the shop-keeper to give me certain things that I wanted, something very spooky happened!! I heard a voice in my right ear saying – "COME BACK", "COME BACK". What you are doing is not needed. I quickly turned back to see that what it was? But there was nothing. I then strangely started walking out of the shop, how should I explain you readers, that moment was hypnotising, I felt that may be someone was calling me and I just came back home. My mind was fully changed. I started thinking that what is the use of making a "house temple", when I will not be able to pray and light the *diya's* – (*diya* – small mud pot mostly in which we pour little oil with cotton ball and light it for praying). As it is I am working where is the time to do all this! No, I should just forget about it. I do believe in God, that more than enough. Basically, I refused to pray and make a "house temple". Friends, this was the sign evil and negative things revolving around me in bulk. They never wanted any pure or sacred thing to be around. Hence, if you have faced or seen anyone behaving like this, refusing to worship, make "house temple", then be scared that something evil has entered that person's life majorly. Beware of this!

I then started calling the property dealers for a new rented accommodation for me. Finally, I got it after three days. I shifted within a week there. This time it was the second floor again! But, different locality!

I was happy, thinking that finally I am out of that 'spooky house' and now things will be all fine here. So, finally I decided to throw a party for all my friends. I invited all of them that weekend! I thought of cooking at home this time and told all my friends that we will be cooking together for fun!! Everyone agreed... I am a Rajput, I used to love chicken, mutton, fish, etc. So, I kept the menu loaded with these recipes. We got all the raw food material alongwith hard-drinks, and my friends started coming one by one. We had loud music, Vodca's, barcardi, wine flowing in the party. Then we distributed work for cooking different non-veg items among us. Someone was chopping onions, garlic, the other was washing chicken and fish, and few were cutting tomato, etc. Full on youngsters party was going on. I decided to make the marination for the mutton. I went to the kitchen and started beating the curd for marination. There was a small window in my kitchen right infront of my cooking range.

Suddenly, I felt that someone was inhailing the smell of raw chicken, fish, mutton which was kept there. I even started feeling that someone was there in my kitchen whom I couldn't see. I called my friends in my kitchen and generally asked that can you feel someone here? She said yes I can feel you, you are standing here infront of me! I laughed it over infront of her and she went out of the kitchen. But I still felt that there was someone around in the kitchen. I then came out to take my barcardi glass and sip in some of the alcohol. I then took the glass of barcardi inside the kitchen, thinking that while cooking I will slowly enjoy its flavour. Again I felt that someone was there, this time I could hear the breathe near my ears also. I quickly ran out of the kitchen, switched off the music system. Everyone looked at me and asked– what happened? why did you stop the music? I said listen guys – There is something strange happening in the kitchen, I think there is something abnormal out there. Everyone entered the kitchen and started looking around, saw the raw non-veg kept there for cooking. They started asking me – what is it? Tell us? we cannot see or feel anything abnormal here. Why are you feeling like this? Just relax Shweta. May be you are too much exhausted with the shifting and managing party stuff. You take it easy and go and sit down with your drink, no need to cook. We will cook for you. And they cheered me up and started the music again. The party was on again!! I went and sat in the drawing room area with my friends and started talking to them generally. I also wanted to enjoy the party. After an hour I felt that someone has come and sat next to me! I looked towards my right there was no one! Now again my mind started giving me signals that what was going on? Why am I feeling such strange things again? Meanwhile, the food got ready and my friends got it on the dinning table. It looked delicious!! All of us pounced on the food!! we were hungry... But I guess I was really, really hungry....!!! Why? I ate more than my normal appetite my friends were looking at me with surprise. They started saying

– Shweta are you Ok? Your eating amount is equivalent to three hungry people! Is the food that tasty or what they asked me? I said I don't know guys but I am unable to stop eating!! I can't say why? Anyway, everyone started eating and enjoying there meal. Hey my readers, I just gave you another symptom of black magic!! Did you gaze it? Yes, I did!! Excess eating, eating more than the normal human diet, either eating too much or not eating at all are important symptoms, of abnormality. Remember this. Lets carry on with the story.....

So then, the party got over. Everyone went back to their houses. But I was still lost in my thoughts of the strange feeling that I had experienced few hours ago in my kitchen area. I was very tired too after the party. Hence, thought of resting on my bed. I laid down on my bed. Suddenly, I felt that someone has climbed on my bed and this time I could feel the bed mattress being pressed with someone's body weight too!! I felt very scared and took the blanket on my face and didn't uttered a word. I understood for sure that there was something wrong around me nor the house that I had shifted. Something really abnormal has trapped me for sure. I started remembering "*Goddess Kali's*" name inside the blanket and slowly I felt that the feeling of someone on my bed started disappearing. I was waiting for the sun rise to take place, before I could even move from my position on the bed. I was damn scared this time... It was sunrise. I came out of my blanket and called "Mr Dash" and told him to come over to my place immediately narrating everything over the phone. He told me not to panic and assured me that he would be there soon. I waited. He finally came after 45 minutes. I told him that happened, I am very much sure now that there is something wrong with me. I am not normal. I feel it strongly. Something soon will not be done then it can get dangerous too take for me too. The moment I finished my sentence, Mr Dash said – Hey dear, how is that possible? You are taking a lot of stress and exhustion these days. Because you stay alone here, your mind is making up all these thoughts and stories. Its psycological problem. Don't worry, you are just Ok. You just need to divert your mind and relax more. There is nothing wrong with you at all. Be assured. Everyone was around last night in the kitchen area and no one felt a thing at all. The reason was because everything was just normal. You have to get out of this phase my dear....

I heard him carefully and with soar throat opened my mouth and said – you are unable to understand my emotions and my situation. I am feeling helpless, alone and misunderstood. This feeling was killing me from within. I felt trapped completely. I started crying as he refused to understand my problem. He tried to console me with his statement but it didn't effect my thought process at all. I told him to leave me alone for sometime....

He followed my instructions and left me, as desired. My readers, here I have to share this with you that it feels really depressed and helpless when you are trapped in this kind of supernatural activity, but nobody believes you because they are unable to experience your terror and fear, that you are going through. Have you ever felt like this in your life? If yes, then you can contact me for sure, because I will definitely believe you, no matter what happens. Atleast you will have one person, that is me, who will understand your trouble, your helplessness and fear for sure. Because, I had gone through the same, but that time no one believed me and there was no one to guide me! But today you have atleast me who will definitely make you believe these weird happenings.

Anyways, lets move on with the rest of the story.... My office work was getting hampered due to all of this. Now, I wanted to get my acts together once again and hit back with a strong sales targets. So, I went to the office and announced in my team that we will achieve double than the mentioned target for the month. Every one was pepped up hearing this in my team, and we got busy with it. Meanwhile, my feeling of someone around me kept on increasing, but now I decided to keep quite and just keep it to myself. Doing all this struggle, almost one month went away.

One day in the morning, when I had off from the office. I was just sitting reading a book alone. I suddenly felt a needle underneath my feet. I pushed back by foot instantly due to the pain of the needle. I looked down on the floor, searching for the needle which might be there on the floor from some one whereas I never used the needle in my house that point of time! But I could not see it! I wondered, what happened to me few seconds back? Could not understand it, so started reading my book again. I love reading books by the way. Again after 10 minutes, I felt the pinch of the needle on my left feet this time! I was unable to see any needle! Suddenly after this, I started feeling sleepy all of a sudden! I just could not stop myself from that sleep and slept... when I woke up after a while and looked down on my feet I was really shocked!! I saw my feet were badly swollen up like small balloons, I got worried. I tried to keep my feet on the floor and walk, but it was very painful for me. My slippers were not fitting me, due to excess swelling. I then remembered that twice I felt a needle being pinned into my feet and it was only after this, my feet got so much swollen. I called up Mr Dash again to narrate the whole thing, he told me to wait, he would take me to the doctor. He again refused to believe that any needle would have pinned my feet! I knew he would not believe, but then I didn't have any choice rather than to narrate this episode to him... We went to the doctor and he saw my feet, and said this is due to exhaustion and not want of sleeping. Gave me the pain-killer and some medicine to subside swelling. Even said it could be due to sudden fluctuation of blood pressure too. We came back. I had started having the medicines from that moment only. Pain did decrease and in a week the swelling also started decreasing. Mr Dash said – "see I told you, that you will be completely fine with regular medicine dozes". I just kept quite. But I knew internally that I did feel the pain from these needles for sure, and there was definitely something related to those needles. But what it was, I could not gather!! After 10 days I became fine. The way all these 'supernatural activities' were happening, similarly, on my professional front, I was thinking of changing my job, for growth and better salary. So I got an internal information regarding "America Express", coming to India, for "Credit Cards" and "Charge Cards", no limit cards. It was shifting its office from "America" to "India" so it will be the international division. They were having recruitments done from a consultant called "Carrier Cruise", in Gurgaon. Offering very handsome salaries and great trainings too. I wanted a brand of "American Express" on my CV and also wanted to learn lot many new things out there. Hence, even I forwarded my CV to the consultant "Carrier Cruise" for getting shortlisted for the interview of "American Express" GIO office situated in Gurgaon.

After 15 days I got a call from "Carrier Cruise", that my CV has been shortlisted for the "Amex" interview. I was really happy. I started preparing myself for the interview day. Then came the interview day. It was held in "Hotel Centurien". The top most cream of all the other Call Center were present there for giving the interview. It was a good competition out there. Everyone looked like quality products!!

Well, the first round of interview started. It was an Ex-tempor round. Different topics were written in a chit, and whichever chit you would pick that topic mentioned inside would be yours!! My topic I remember was – "If Monkeys were team leaders and Chimpanzees were managers, what would you like yourself to be in that organisation and why?" Hmm.... The moment I got this topic, and I read it loud, everyone present out there started laughing... Then I started, my Ex-tempor. My answer was like this :–

If monkey's were team leaders and chimpanzees were managers in an organisation, then I would want myself to be a human, because human has the brains to control the monkeys and chimpanzees and make sure that they do what is required for them to do. Thats about it.

Hearing this, the HR executive smiled and I was send for the second round. Like this there were live more rounds which needed to be clarified before meeting the HR manager of Amex "Mr Jyoti Brata" for the last salary round!! I got a call from the organisation after a week that I had to go for my last and final round of interview to "Hotel Marriot". I went there, met "Mr Jyoti Brata", he was a gem of a person. Very polite focussed, good analyser and very intelligent of course. He asked me few questions and then finally said to me – "I would like to offer you the employment of American Express, will you accept it"? I smiled and said – "Yes, Mr Brata, I would love to, thank you".

He wished me good luck and handed over the LOI (Letter of Intend). I was very happy. Because, now I would be working for the world's best customer service brand – "American Express"!!

I came back home and called my friends and told them about this new employment of mine. Everyone was very happy for me!!

Finally the day came, the first day we were to reach. "Hero Mind Mine" Gurgaon for induction. I reached, our Induction happened. We were divided into different groups for training. One month of pre- process training or you may call it "Voice and Accent Training". Second month of "Process- Training". Third months of "OJT" meaning ON the job-training. All these three stages needed to be certified. Three months just passed by, with plenty of hard work and exams, certifications, learnings, etc. Alongwith, all of this my statue problems of the 'supernatural activities' also started getting bigger day by day. I started feeling the presence of somebody all the time with me even in the office. I was mentally really disturbed but no one was ready to subscribe my views. So, I used to throw myself badly into work and started doing over-time, double shifts etc. I never felt like going back home. Everyone in my office used to think that I am workoholic. But the truth was that I was trying to escape from the "unknown"!!

One day as usual I was coming to the office in the cab, and again I felt the needle being pinned behind my ears and then the next what I understood was – someone was waking me up. Few voices I could hear which said –"wake up Shweta, wake up". Then few drops of water I could feel on my face. Suddenly, I woke up and saw that there were 10-12 people outside the cab and one person was trying to wake me up! They told me I had fainted on the way, when? Even they did not realise, when? I just couldn't understand a thing that point of time!! Somehow, my collegues helped me to get out of the cab and supported me to reach till the floor area. I reached to my desk and had a glass of water. One of my friends got me a cup of coffee too, alongwith chocolate to eat, thinking that may be it was due to low B.P. that I had fainted. I was really confused about everything that was happening at that point of time. Still I continued with my work slowly. The shift got over. I reached back home. I was really tired and felt asleep. Suddenly, after sometime I once again felt the needle being pinned on my hands, fingers, neck, head everywhere with more force this time. I started shouting with pain. Nothing stopped!! Then I called my friend on the phone and she came running from nearby only. She saw me and my condition. She wanted to take me to her house to her mom, but before she could arrange for it, I again fainted!!

Next, when I opened my eyes I was in the hospital. I saw my friend standing near me along with her mother. My needle pain was over. She told me that everything has come out to be normal as per the doctor. Now I can leave. May be it was due to weakness and work load, that I fainted. I was quite. We left from the hospital, came back to my friends place. She told me to stay there with her that night, seeing my condition, so I also agreed. After dinner, I came to her room and we sat down together with a cup of coffee. She asked me too tell her everything that was going on in my life in length, without any hesitation. I bursted into tears infront of my friend and narrated the whole episode right from the starting.

After hearing my whole story very carefully and actively my friend holded my hand and consoled me truely. Then she said to me – "Shweta now whatever I am going to say to you please try to understand it carefully". Then she says that the matter that you have just narrated to me is very sensitive and dangerous. If all this is true then you are in big trouble my friend. And I know that the people around you who claim to be highly educated and sophisticated will refuse to believe in it completely. Which means that now you will have to face this alone with strong will-power and the faith to be healed. When no one is ready to stand with you, then that time its your faith and believe that can sail you through from the most difficult situations also. So be brave". This was my friends motivational therapy for me!!

And yes, trust me it wasn't just a speech for me, but was the most important lesson that I had learned in my life. Yes, she was right. When nothing works then faith does work. My friend was staying here with her parents. We decided that she would help me with this matter now. I was a bit relieved that finally I have someone who is ready to understand my feelings and pain. Next day, we were to go to some "spiritual healer" known to her. I got ready and she took me to that healer. He told us to come the next day, saying he will look into the matter in the night. We came back. When we reached back home, my friend's father had very high-fever all of a sudden and was vomiting repeatedly. We rushed to the hospital and he was admitted there. Doctor said he has to be kept under observation, so that it should not turn into the brain fever. I had to come back to my house. Next day, when I called up my friend to ask her that how was her father and how about going to the healer as he had called us the next day? She shouted badly at me and said— don't call me ever again, I don't want to take you anywhere at all!! Leave me alone, its because of you that my father is not well, and she disconnected the call!! I was really shocked and very angry also. Why the hell is she blaming things on me? How dare she accused me for something that I have not done? This feeling was irritating me from within, hence I decided to call her up from my friends cell number as she was disconnecting my calls frantically. Then from the unknown cell number she picked up my call!!

And I said to her – "Listen whatever you just said few hours ago I just could not understand a bit of it too! But, yes, what I do understand is that you are talking completely senseless and just blaming me for something that I have no relations with. The way you spoke with me was aweful, and don't need your help or asistance in anything from now. Infact, I don't want to have you as my friend any more myself. So, it is just over between you and me forever. Do hell with you and your stupid blame game".... And I disconnected the call this time...

I felt little relieved after giving it back to my friend at that point of time, because she was blaming me for something that I had not done! After that she never called me nor I got interested to speak with her ever again!! That friendship got over forever...

Have you lost your dear friend like this ever? Have you ever faced uneccessary fights between you and your known ones? Have you been accused for things that you have not even thought of going away from the person who always used to stand by you in your hardships? Well, if yes, then take a minute off and think – was it natural, or was it planned against you guys? Planned, so that your support system, unity, should break. Because someone wants to see you alone without your people around you, so that no help should be able to reach to you!!

This was exactly that was happening with me that time. Yes, intentionally misunderstandings were getting created around me and my dear ones, slowly and slowly my social circle started fading away. I started having fights with my good friends infact I never wanted to be with many people.

Anyway, then as I mentioned it earlier before that I had a fight with my friend who wanted to take me to her healer for knowing my present condition hence, I did not approach the healer him after any feedback after that. So, there I was again loneliness, helplessness and mentally tensed about what next will happen to me now?

Day by day my health started getting affected. I started fainting in the cabs while travelling to the office every now and then! My mind was always in the fear of seeing or facing the unknown. I started getting irritated on small things around me! My blood pressure used to be mostly low. My health was giving me major signals about something being major wrong with me! But I was unable to do anything about it. My reports in the doctors clinic or hospitals came out to be absolutely normal. But my body was under different types of aches and weakness.

While all of this was happening with me, one thing was getting very strongly developed inside me! It was the curiosity of knowing about this unknown world— 'supernatural world'! Yes, now I had started feeling that I have to accept the fact that I am trapped, in some way or the other in this 'Paranormal' activity. Hence, there has to be a way out also for this. Now, I have to find the way out of this!!

So, one fine day, I decided alone, that now I will fight back. Yes, I will not just sit in fear and apprehension now. I will create a will-power which helps me to find out a cure for my problem. Now, I will not make a joke out of myself, asking people to help me in this matter anymore. Because no one was believing on me as well!

It was only me who feels it, its only me who used to sense it and it was only me who was getting all the physical pains and suffering alongwith the mental pain. No one else was going through it! So I only have to get out of it with dignity. Hence, now I decided not to even mention my problem to any new or old contact of mine....

But this decision became like a curse for me! Yes, curse is the word most appropriate. Because with each day passing by, my pain in the body, my feeling of being with someone whom cannot see at all but feel for sure kept on increasing. It was very scary and horrible, being all alone. But now come, what may. I will not surrender to the demands of any fear around me, took my pledge.

Infact now within myself, in my conscious I had started challenging the evil forces which had trapped me, that I know you are there to kill me, I cannot see you, but I do feel your presence around me. You are powerful, you are scary, but you cannot defeat me till the time I give up on myself. So will hold on! Yes, I will hold on!

Even when so much was happening with me, I did not loose hope, I still was waiting for someone, for that one person who will agree to my situation and help me to get out of this 'Supernatural' activity. Somewhere down the line, I knew that there was some power which was saving me, despite so many of evil forces being around me....

So guys/gals never let your will power die. Never let your desire to live die! never let your faith and believe die, because only strong determination will help you to come out of the strongest from of 'Black Magic' practises also. How? You will surely get to know in my story later....

Lets continue... So as I had explained above that my health had started getting from bad to worse. I decided to resign from "American Express", with dignity and take rest. Everyone in "Amex" wanted me to stay there, and go on a medical leave, before resigning all of a sudden like this. They were very supportive and nice. But I knew that no medical leave will cure my disease that early. Infact Mr. Brata told me that I would join back once fit! I really thanked him from the bottom of my heart for showing the deep concern for me. He asked me several times that I could share my views or any problem with him. May be something works for me!! But I humbly said there was nothing to share! Its just my health issue! Because as I said that I had taken the pledge of not opening my mouth infront of anybody! Finally, I was out from "Amex" on my own!! I started staying back at home for resting more. I used to sleep a lot. Eat a lot, and just tried to digest the pain that I was getting into my body through needles! Now everyday, I kept on praying in my conscious that God please send me someone, who understands this pain that I am presently going through....

After a long wait of two months something new happened. "Mr Dash" decided to organise a get together of his friends at my place, so that even my mood changes a bit.

I agreed as usual like a fool!! Fool because I never knew that he was the main culprit behind my present situation!! Anyway all his friends came on time, there was one new face among them! I asked his name and his reason for visiting Delhi, because he said he stayed in Calcutta and came Delhi for getting a job. Basically, he had shifted his base alone to Delhi for building up his carrier in computer field. He was a "Web-Designer". But his native place was in Bihar. After knowing all this from him, I introduced myself to him. Told him about myself, my corporate field, etc. There was something very strange about this chap! What it was, I could not gather at that very moment! But I wanted to meet him again! I liked his presence. Strangely, I felt for the first time, that may be he believes in all these 'supernatural' activities existing and may be he will be able to understand my problem too!! Reason, for me to think like that. I didn't know why I am tousing on this line.....

But, it was our first meeting. I never would like to start any conversation with a stranger, as I took a pledge not to share my problems with anybody. So the party went on fine, as usual for me it was just the same story of pain and discomfort all the time. But it was just that I was pretending to be normal and fine! Finally, the party got over, everyone went back to their houses.

After three days, I started getting horrifying dreams I could not sleep. Sometimes I used to see water flood, sometimes skulls and bones around me in dreams, sometimes see myself without hair on my head and etc.,.... Now, my sleep also started getting affected. Another issue started in my life, where as I was already in so much of trouble! One night I was standing in my house balcony, unable to sleep, around 12.30 in the night and I just feel like jumping from the balcony all of a sudden! The feeling was very strong, and I had moved my one foot ahead also. But then something stopped me and I came inside immediately. I got really scared that night.

The next morning I woke up quite disturbed due to last night's abnormal activity. I went to the kitchen for making lime and honey water for myself. Suddenly, there was a door bell sound. I went to open the door. To my surprise what I saw? The new guy in the group that I told before came to my house!! I was really shocked yet happy to see him. I asked him about him urpase of visiting? He replied back saying, Mr Dash has called me here for some business planning! I said that Mr Dash never informed me about anything like this... Anyway you can come in and wait for him for sure. I offered him a hot cup of tea. We were just sitting together and waiting for Mr Dash to come. I called him to ask, that whether you have called your friend over today for some business planning? He said, yes, I have but somehow it skipped from my mind to tell this to you I am really very sorry! I said, its Ok, when are you reaching here? He said it would take one hour atleast, and we finally disconnected the call.

I informed the new guy that he would be here in an hour's time. We sitting and talking tea together. I thought, that now it is a good time to ask him about my doubts and know about his perceptions regarding 'supernatural' things existing. Let me check whether he believes in all these things or not. I questioned him directly – "Do you believe in 'supernatural' things"? He was shocked, his face became blank all of a sudden. He said what? I repeated myself – "Do you believe in 'supernatural' things"? He asked me – why are you asking this kind of question to me? I replied – Because I want to know, its important for me to know...

He finally said – Yes, I do believe. Infact I have seen all of these 'supernatural' activities happening in Calcutta a lot of times. People do 'Black Magic' to achieve their targets commonly in various parts of the world. Yes, there is a way to trap any human being into abnormal activities. All these things I believe in because I have seen many people around me getting trapped into it, infront of my own eyes!! I was shocked hearing this detail from him. Finally, I had someone infront of my eyes, who at least confidently admitted this existence of 'Paranormal' activities!!

Then came a question from his side. But why do you want to know about this? I was quite. He said please tell me, I am also curious to know. I looked at him, deep into his eyes and said – "Because I am trapped completely into the 'supernatural' activities myself, "but no one believes me". Hence, I had thought of keeping quite about it.

He was stunned hearing this from me. He said – Are you joking? I said – No, I am not, I am very serious, its the truth of my life. I need help, I need someone to believe me, and help me to come out of this big unknown, unseen problem. I am dying every second with fear, pain, mental torture. But no one understands me. When I looked at you, I really don't know, what told me within me that may be you believe in all these 'supernatural' things existing. Hence, asked you this question. And see, I was right also, you do know about these things existing....

He became quite with surprise. He asked me – what do you want from me now? I said, I want you to guide me, how to come out of this miserable phase which shattered my life, I am suffering each minute here. He then asked me – "Ok, please tell me in detail about how this started and what all you have faced till now"? I started narrating everything to him right from the starting till that very moment. Once I had finished my narration his face looked scared, confused and at the same time he had sympathy in his eyes for me. Yes, I could see that.

You people must be thinking that how desperately I felt relieved for a while by narrating my whole sufferings to him!! But you don't know my friends, how exactly a victim feels at that point of time? He/she just wants to get back their normal life.

I also told him that "Mr Dash" doesn't believe in all these hence please don't mention anything to him about all of this. He agreed. I told him listen, you are like a brother to me, please help me. He told me, I can understand your pains and suffering but even I have to take a very strong and hard decision regarding my loyalities towards my friend. Because I know you through Mr Dash. Hence, if I support you, indirectly I will be hurting my friend also. This thought is stopping me to say, yes, to you. On the other hard, whatever you just narrated to me, if that is actually true, then it will be unfair on my part to avoid or ignore your helplessness and pain!! I am really very confused at this point of time. Please just give me some quality time to think about it and so that I can take the correct decision.... I agreed and somewhere down my heart respected his answer and feelings that he had for "Mr Dash".

Meanwhile, Mr. Dash also arrived! I left both these men alone in the drawing room and came inside into my room. They finished their business planning session and left together. Slowly, the attacks were as it is increasing on me, I had started looking ill now. I even started getting irritated on small things, started hating the light of the sun. One day, I took the blackchart papers and covered all my room windows with it, so that not even a single ray of sunlight should enter my room. My child like charm, chirpiness, my happy nature, positive nature was dying very fast now.... My hair fall started, my financial condition definitely was getting destroyed as I was unable to work, due to my health problems. I had even reached a point, where I was scared to go to the washroom in the night, felt frightened to roam in my own house, people around me now could sense that there was something terribly wrong with me! All of this was getting noticed by this new friend of Mr Dash, too. But I never asked him for help after that day because he had asked me for some quality time to think about the matter.

One afternoon, I and this new friend were sitting in the

drawing room and he all of a sudden said to me – "Shweta I have decided, I will surely help you in your supernatural matter". I have seen that you are really suffering a lot, and now I genuinely want to support you to come out of this 'supernatural' stuff. The moment I heard this, I felt happy. And I looked at him to thank him for showing the concern. But something very unusual and unexpected happend!! When I looked at him my face was not looking normal. Yes, my reader I had an abnormal look on my face, my eyes were little yellow in colour and my voice became heavy and I said – "You will help me to come out of black magic?" and I smilled wickedly after that!! The friend of mine got up from the couch instantly and started enchanting. *"Goddess Kali's mantras"*, looking at me. And within five minutes, I became normal and fainted after that.

When I opened my eyes, I saw this guy sitting next to me and splashing some water on my face to wake me up....

I sat down. He asked me, whether I was feeling Ok? I answered in my normal voice, yes I am Ok. Then he told me that today he has got the biggest proof regarding me being trapped in the 'supernatural' activity infront of him only. And he would never forget this site ever. He said to me – From today onwards you are my little sister and now I will do everything possible to bring you out of this 'Paranormal' thing.

I felt nice after hearing this and thanked God for finally sending a helping hand for me. He assured me that things will soon get back to normal. That day both of us took a pledge, that we will not give up infront of any hurdle or fright which will be created to stop us from getting out of this 'Supernatural' trap. He told me that now I had to be very strong to fight back. And I agreed with him on this....

Hey! dear readers, now the turning point of my life has started from here. Turning point because now I refused to be a victim any more and, decided to fight back and get back my normal life from all these negativities around me. So here is a lesson for all those who are suffering from any kind of 'Black Magic' or 'Supernatural' activity. Refuse to be a victim from within yourself and create a will power to face the negativity and heal yourself through professional genuine help. Have faith in almighty, and you will definitely feel the difference. Because that's exactly what I had done, and yes it did worked for me!! How? Lets begin....

Our first step towards betterment took place. The step was calling up my parents and informing them about my 'supernatural' problem, urgently!! Yes, my friends, this was very important because I needed that support system behind me for sure. Now, I would like to disclose that guys name infront of all, who was ready to help me through this matter. His name was Neeraj. I have taken permission from him to disclose his name in public!! Because my idea is to show you readers, that everything out here is genuine. So lets continue...

Neeraj and I finally decided to call my parents. I was very reluctant in doing so, because I had fought with them because of "Mr Dash", and left the house. But Neeraj convinced me that, no, this step was actually important, no matter how much scolding or scuffs I have to face. That would be very natural on my families part! Because ultimately they have also felt hurt with this conduct of mine. I agreed completely with this thought.

So, then I finally called up my mom with lot of courage. She picked the call. I told her everything over the phone, in detail. She was really shocked and surprised till the core! She told me to come back to my parents house leaving everything behind. She promised me that no one would say a word to me in my house. Infact, she said to me that she had this hint within herself that something is not normal about my behaviour. That's why I had left my house, she added. She was sure about this, that I have been trapped in 'Black Magic' by somebody to destroy my life completely! I was really zapped after hearing my mother's view points! The reason was, I kept on begging and pleading infront of everyone for believing in my 'supernatural' trouble that I was facing but, no one took me seriously, and here, just once I spoke to my mother and she was ready to help me!! I was really touched by this gesture and finally I went to my house to meet my family. All of them were waiting for me to come there. The moment I entered my house, they were surprised to see me! My mom said "What is wrong with you"? You look so pale ! Infact you look as if you are ill! Your eyes are yellowish in colour, you are looking so very weak. I sat down. Had tea. Narrated everything infront of my mom, dad and brother. They were really shocked hearing each and every detail from me. They said to me that why I didn't informed them earlier about so much happening in my life? I said because I was so scared and nervous about the fact that you people will mad at me and not believe me because I fought and left the house for "Mr Dash". They told me that they never wanted me to go through any kind of misery in future, hence were just stopping me to get into any trouble. I was first quite.

Then I told them about Neeraj that he suggested me to contact my parents and family. My mom told me to call Neeraj home immediately. She wanted to meet him and discuss few things. So, I called him and he reached my house.

There my family members and Neeraj had a long conversation about my narration on 'supernatural' activities faced by me. They also specified "Mr Dash" in that conversation and my mom told him that she finds this character very fishy! And you must keep a strong eye on him and his activities too, being his friend. And all of us decided that I should pack my bags and come back to my family today itself.

I went to my rented accommodation where I had shifted all alone packed my bags and came back to my house, without informing "Mr Dash" or anyone.

In the evening "Mr Dash" called me up generally! I told him that I have returned to my parents house. The moment he heard this, instead of being happy for me, he shouted *back very badly on me saying*—"How dare I took this step without informing him"? I was really zapped by his behaviour and tone! I yelled back at him saying — "Don't you dare to raise your voice with me like this" and I disconnected the call. I really feel very bad that moment.

But at the same time I felt good that I was back in my house in my own room, had my mom's homecooked delicious food and then peacefully watched TV after a very long time! I was happy also. The feeling of coming back to your own house cannot be expressed in words. It can just be felt and treasured within. It was 1.30 in the night and I had gone off to sleep, after a long time in my own familiar bed!

Suddenly, I woke up in haste... I felt that something really chilled is kept on my felt! I looked down, there was nothing. There was a window in my room, I felt that from there something chilled entered my room. I stared at that window, but I could not see anyone as I said before also. But I could feel for sure that there was something out there. My feet started getting extremely cold and numb, only my feet! This point is to be noted very carefully! I tried to move myself out of the bed, but my feet unable to move. I then somehow tried to shout out loud to call my mom or brother from the other room. But I failed here. My voice was chocked! Yes, its true, I was unable to speak. Now, the only option I had was to crawl like an animal and reach to the door of my mom or brother's room. So I tried doing it! I went to my mom's bedroom door and started banging the door with my one hand. She opened the door and looked infront of the door. She could not see me, because I was crawling down! Then I pulled her maxi that she had worn with my hand and then she looked down. She got after scared seeing me. She switched on the light immediately and asked me what happened?

I was unable to speak as I mentioned before. She quickly banged my brother's door and he came out, seeing me like this even he got scared. Both of them pulled me upwards and somehow managed to put me on the bed. My mom gave me "Ganges holy water" to drink. (It is supposed to be a holy water from river Ganges in India). My head was burning with very high temperature and I was shivering at the same time. My brother rushed downstairs to call the doctor who was staying in the society only.

The doctor came in the emergency situation. He checked me and he was puzzled, because the thermometer showed no temperature at all. And my body was burning with high fever. All of them were shocked seeing my condition. Suddenly, I got my voice back. I shouted—*"Hanuman Chalisa"* read it. My mom immediately gave it to my brother he started reading it loudly. The moment he started reading it loudly, my legs started going into upward motion! I started holding my legs so that they remain straight but, I could not succeed. Then my mom and doctor had to pull my legs strongly so that they remain steady. I was going upwards from my leg area. My body was rising above from the bed and my mom and doctor had to put lot of strength to get me back on the bed. Suddenly, I became OK and I fainted. My temperature came back to normal. My legs were fine. I was not shivering. After 15-20 minutes, I woke up and I was normal. But mom's face and my brother's face were blank! That night they had seen me in such a precarious situation and my 'supernatural' activity with their own eyes, too. Now they were hundred per cent sure that I was trapped badly and dangerously in the grip of some 'Black Magic' act. They made me sleep after that and said that we will discuss in detail about this next morning. They were kept themselves awake the whole night and made me sleep in peace! This can be expected only by those, who really care for you.....

I woke up in the morning. My mom and my brother offered me tea and biscuits. My mom said that now it is proved having after went through last night episode, you are under the grip of 'supernatural' effects. Now, we will have to take appropriate steps to get you out of this horrific stage. I could see the tension and worries in my mom's eyes.

Meanwhile "Mr Dash" was calling me you frantically, but I was not taking his calls at all, I was very weak and irritated with his behaviour too.

Next night also I experienced more problems as I started seeing shadows around me. They were walking in a circle, I was in the middle. I shouted badly and my mom and brother came running out in my room. They could not see anything! But they realised that whatever I was saying was correct. Those shadows disappeared after my family members entered my room. My dad had gone out of town for some business work. Next morning he arrived. Everything was told to him in detail as well.

He immediately said—"I will go and find out *Guruji*". You are thinking who is that Guruji. I have not mentioned about him before! Yes, the reason was, because he had gone for his meditation and *Sadhana* for a long time. But now my brother and father went to check him whether he had come back or not!

It was my good luck that Guruji was back. He told my brother and dad that why they had come to him? My dad told him that they were there for me! He told them that it would take 12 days for him to cure me from 'Black Magic'. Till that 12 days he would not see my face nor he would talk to me. All the details, who did it what exactly it was, would be explained later when I would be out of this trouble... Hearing this they came back home hoping for the best! They narrated me everything and my mom. After hearing I felt good, somewhere deep in my heart I knew that now I will be cured for sure.

As *Guruji* said 12 days will take for curing me. Each day went by with negative vibration being removed and I used to feel better exactly the place from where those needles or pins on the putla or Doll were getting removed. I used to tell my mom and brother that right now from this particular area it was seen removed! Twelve days passed by. On the thirteen days day, I feel absolutely energetic and fine. The yellow colours from my eyes had disappeared, my body was out from weakness. *Guruji* had called my brother and father on the given date to disclose the truth. They went to meet him again.

Guruji said— "One pin in the Putla or Doll is sufficient to destroy one human-being," here there were 1000 pins iereed on her Putla or Doll how could she survive for all these months? I failed to understand it. Then I checked it through my *"Sadhana Shakti"* and found, *"Goddess Kali"*, is with her, saving her from those evil spirits. Otherwise, she would have died by now for sure.

Yes, *Guruji* said—Her Putla or Doll was made and 1000 needles were pinned in it. That was the reason that she used to feel the needles getting pinned on her skin for real. There were "1000 *jinns*" that had surrounded her. All of them were making her weak and kept her unhealthy. That's why she used to feel that evil spirits are with her all the time, but unable to see them!! Her blood circulation was stop ped by these needles. But, now, she is completely OK ! She is now out of danger and will get back her nomality soon.

But onething I want to tell you, *Guruji* said— "she had been under the influence of *"Vashikaran"* also. There is a guy, who had done this *"Vashikaran"* on her to get her in him life and let her be away from her family, that is why she fought with her own family and left the house. It was not her fault. She was given a very dirty things to eat, for the *"Vashikaran"* to be implemented on her !! Hence, it is my order that no one would scold her over this or trouble her regarding the topic of that guy ever. She went through a lot. I do not want to see her in more pain" !!

The next immediate question was asked to *Guruji* soon after hearing this. Who did all this *Guruji*? He was furiously answered — "The same guy for whom she left the house— Mr Dash"!! My family members were in shocked to hear all of this! Then *Guruji* added— "Mr Dash" did *"Vashikaran"* on her through some *"Tantric"* and his mother had put 1000 *jinns* on her to kill her, so that her son doesn't think of her and leave her forever. As it doesn't leads to any fight and due to this process of course she will have to leave this world. Hence, automatically this relation which is growing deep will end. So basically, Mr Dash wanted her to be in his life, but her mother did not agree to this, and wanted her completely out of his life. But at the same time, his mother never wanted to show her true colours infront of her son. She wanted to be in his good books only, hence she opted for 'Black Magic'. As her motive will be achieved without spoiling the relation with of her son. He also added that you can call "Mr Dash" infront of me and I will say it on his face that yes his mother was responsible for this 'Black Magic' that Shweta had gone through!! My brother immediately said— Yes, *Guruji* that will be good thing to do. Lets do this. All of them agreed.

When I was told all of this truth after they returned home, I was mumbers and disheartened! Because my trust was shaken completely. I was feeling cheated and betrayed. Firstly, hearing that Mr Dash had done *Vashikaran* on me and then hearing the second thing about his mother, that she wanted to get me out from his life and even wanted to kill me!! I was really taken aback after knowing all of this. I trusted my *Guruji* completely. Now, I could relate to all the past incidences that is why Mr Dash always tried to ignore this when I used to tell him about my feeling of sensing someone around me and all the other attacks and fears. Mr *Dash* never ready to accept this and tried to pacify me that these were not true. That was the reason that I said 'yes' to him, while I was completely against him before. Now each and every picture was clear to me. I got my acts together and decided to call Neeraj and told him about the truth now. I also wanted to see that will Mr Dash accept all of these things or not?

I called up Neeraj, and told him everything that *Guruji* had disclosed. He was shocked and very angry at the same time. We finally called Mr Dash to my place. My parents, my brother, Neeraj and I were there. I told him all of this. He very smartly said that I would only believe all of this when your *Guruji* would come and say me directly. I knew he would say something like this for sure! Next day, *Guruji* came for ten minutes, because he we always very busy with his clients. Mr Dash was also present there.

Guruji pointed a finger and looked towards Mr Dash with anger and said— your mother had put 1000 *jinns* on her. Now I saved her, she is cured, I even left your mother without harming her this time but if next time anything like this gets repeated ever then I won't spare her spiritually. Remember this. If you want to ask me any question about this matter then ask right now, I will answer! I still remember Mr Dash's face. He was shocked, nervous, and blank. Guruji again asked him the same thing, and this time he replied— No I don't have any doubts or questions. He looked depressed after hearing all of this. *Guruji* left after blessing meand family.

I looked at Mr Dash and he was on the verge of crying! I told him that it is very difficult for me to forget all this that

Guruji just mentioned and even your rude conduct that I faced Hence, it is better that you leave now. He started apologising to me after this. He begged to any mother and said that he doesn't want me to leave. But I had decided that I had to get rid of these people for sure. Hence, I told him that now there is nothing left, its better we end this relation mutually. He left after hearing this....

So, my dear readers, has anything like this happened with any one of you which I faced? Or may be someone that you know have ever talked about these things that I have mentioned here? If 'yes' then you must take that person seriously, you never know he/she would be heading towards the ends very soon!! Hence, wake up and the least you can do is, tell them to contact a 'Paranormal' expert or spiritual healer, before it gets too late!!

Anyway, my sordid saga doesn't ends here! Nor my sufferings got over completely! How? You must be wondering that just few minutes back, I said that I had got totally cured by the blessings of my *Guruji*, then which other sufferings I am referring to? Lets begin another very important chapter of my life... So as I mentioned just that I had said a good-bye to Mr Dash forever and even all the sufferings of 'Black Magic' created by him and his mother. Now, was the time for me to think about my own self, to start all over again.

In my previous take, I did mention about my passion for "Civil Service"! Yes it is, "Civil Service". I had planned right from my school days to pursure my career in this line. Hence, I used to be all the time preparing my handwriting, speed of writing, choosing the correct subjects etc according to the future plan for 'Civil Service' exam!! But as you all know by now, that how I got lost mid=way to lose my hard earned money and it was due to Mr. Dash game plan etc....

Then I thought, now things have come back to normal. My last year of college was over too. I did my graduation in "Pol-Science 'Hons'." Now, I could join an institute which prepares for civil services examination. Then I chose an institute which is situated in "Connught Place, New Delhi", a very famous one. I went there for getting admission. They fee there was Rs 50,000 for prelims. I had decided that I would pay the fee from my own savings that I had made after working in the Call Center. So, I deposited that amount from my own pocket. My parents were also happy with this decision. My mother called up my grandmother to inform about my health. She told her that now. I was out of black-magic completely and narrated her everything that had happened to me in length. She also informed my grandmother about my decision to take admission in a "Civil Service institute". My grandmother was very happy hearing this and thanked Almighty for saving my life from such a danger. My mother also informed her own sister about my story. Everybody was shocked after hearing this! But they were all happy to hear that now I was preparing for "civil services" examination.

So, after three days my batch for civil services was started. I was all very excited for going to the institute meeting new people, being among the intelligent group etc... Finally that day had come. I reached the institute, I was guided towards my classroom there by a coordinator. I could see students from all parts of India. Everyone got a common dream of bevoming "IAS, IPS, IFS officer"!! I could see a very healthy competition all around me. It was a very emotional moment for me also ! Yes, emotional because I could see that few students from lower middle class background also, but somehow had the courage to apply for such dignified and tough examinations, along with submitting the exhorbitant fees of Rs 50,000 too! How they would have managed it? It also showed me a way that how one must think big and dream big. How much they must be struggling to be in Delhi, a place which is expensive to stay and survive, especially for students who are coming from small towns with poor ecommic background. This was the first time that I was emotional about others rather than thinking of partying and spending money unnecessarily. I realised that seeing death so closely made me sensitive towards other people!!

While I was thinking all of this, our professor entered the classrooms. All of us wished him with respect and his introductions about himself and the institute started. He also mentioned about having an back-up future option, rather than just being an "IAS officer" because according to him its good to facus your target for clearing civil services examination, but its also important to understand that only few candidates would be able to clean it. Not everybody could be an "IAS" hence all of us should keep an alternate option in mind too, and must not get into the depression phase if we are unable to clear the "civil services" exam! Because it needs 50 per cent of luck and 50 per cent of hard work to achieve this position. I really got inspired after hearing my professors speech and teachings.

Then another professor came and explained about the GK paper etc. The whole day went by, like this. Then, I came back home. The day was productive, I got to know about "civil services examination pattern much more closely.

The next morning again I reached the institute on time. That day was about taking down notes from different professors, their teachings to be grasped attentively. Suddenly, after one hour in the class while writing my notes in my register, my fingers of the hand started shivering and my ring finger of my right-hand started giving me a lot of pain. I was unable to hold the pen properly. I had to stop writing. I was unable to understand what was happening to me at that time. I was trying to concentrate on the professors lecture. But this pain of my fingers was not letting me concentrate completely! After 15 minutes a very bad headache also started near my temples! Now, this was the limit of my tolerance power. I told my professor that I wasn't feeling well and had asked his permission to put my head down on the desk itself and was listening to his lectures carefully. The class got ever. Everyone in the class came to me to ask, whether I was Ok? I said, I am just not feeling well! They all advised me to return home and took some rest for the day. I had no other option except listening to all the students. Hence, I came back home in a cab. My mother was surprised to see me back early! She asked me how could return so early? I told her see my hand, its shivering and my finger is under lot of pain along with a very bad headache also. I just wanted to lie down in my room. She gave me some water to drink. Around in the evening, I felt that as if few needles were getting inserted on my head area, exactly where the brain is situated! Now, I remembered the 'Black Magic' symptom that I had recently faced. It started paining bally. I shouted and called my brother and mother. And very told them that needles are getting pinned in my head area... Even they got shocked, once again hearing after the same words from me!!

My mother called up *Guruji* immediately and informed him about me. *Guruji* said he will look into the matter straight away. After speaking to *Guruji*, that needles pain stopped within an hour's time! I slept, woke up straight in the morning. Got ready, and reached my institute as usual. I had thought that today I would cover up for yesterday's also, took down notes, that were missed by me after to day,s class.

Professor came, the class started. I was Ok, for two hours. Soon after that my hand felt that someone was hitting it with a hammer or a similar weapon! I started shouting in the class. My professor came running to my desk and asked what happened? I told him the same as I mentioned earlier. He and everyone in the class were zapped hearing it!! They said—what the hell are you saying Shweta ? How is this possible? I said, yes its possible, its called 'Black Magic'! I had earlier suffered from it also! Everyone was unable to understand what I just said.... I knew that I was just wasting my time, trying to explain them my position ! Hence, I decided to just run away from there. So, I got up from my seat and ran outside from the class room. Everybody was shocked seeing me, I never turned back to look at them I knew they would be thinking of me to be absolutely psycho. But my past experience had taught me one good thing regarding 'Black Magic'—If you are trapped in 'Black Magic', you don't have to waste your energies in proving it to others instead you should just think of getting yourself cured without wasting any time. So, I followed my past experience. I sat in my cab quickly and told the driver to just rush back home!!

I entered the house with major pain and helplessness. I knew that this was the same known pain and suffering. My mom came to me and again lighted the *"Puja Diya"* infront of *"Maa Kali"* and started praying for my betterment. My brother tried to contact my *Guruji* once again, over the phone. But *Guruji* was not available on the phone... Hence, now was the time to fight with will power and strong faith!! So I started looking at *Goddess Kali*'s photo and praying that please get me out of this pain, I am your true devotee and have faith in you, help me *Maa Kali,* help me please, you must not let this demon or evil forces overpower me. This was the inner-voice from me and with true heart and desire. After one and half hours, the pain vanished automatically! I was still sitting infront of Goddess *Kali* and asking for her protection and courage. Then I got up and narrated the whole classroom episode to my mother in detail. She knew after hearing this that again some kind of 'Black Magic' attacked me, but what kind of 'Black Magic' it could be, when everything had been sorted out by *Guruji* recently!! Such questions were going on in my mind, but no answer was coming out!!

After 4-5 hours later, I saw suddenly my feet were turning blue in colours, very light blue like of the sky colour and started swelling up too, then the pain started getting into my legs, upward motion and even the bluish colour started travelling towards my leg. I shouted and called my mother and brother! Even they were shocked after seeing this. Then, suddenly, I felt a snake around me and told my mom that it seeme someone pruned has planted some poison for me this time through 'Black Magic' process, because I could sense a snake poison and its presence very strongly. Now, I started feeling sleepy also and my legs were turning blue with fast pace. My mother tied a strong cloth around my leg so that the poison should not travel upwards. She kept on telling me that don't sleep Shweta but I just remembered "Lord Shiva" and snake around his neck and just said that please save me "Lord Shiva", I know that this process is something to do with the snake's poison. And saying this I slept. I don't know what happened after that. But when I woke up my mother and brother were sitting next to me only and my legs got alright once again and even the swelling went away!! My mother told me that when I last night after that episode the bluish colour started fading was sleeping gradually along with the swelling. Now this was again a miracle!! Only I could feel this, and of course cannot give any scientific explanation for this, nor I can have a proof of this! But, yes, this was the truth that I had experienced.

It was important for me to mention these happenings here because, my mission is to make everyone aware that yes, such things do happen with several people and only they know about it and it cannot be scientifically proved or assessed. But, yes these things do exists. Well, infact let me ask you people, that has anyone experienced something similar to this? If yes then you will be able to relate to this episode very easily. And if no, then hey, you are very much lucky dear !!

Anyway I want to leave this on you people only and lets move forward with the continuation of the truth....

Immediately after this, the door bell was ringing. My mother opened the door and saw one of my relatives at the door. Who came from Chandigarh, without making a call or informing us, they arrived! My mother and me were shocked seeing them all of a sudden. Infact, the first thing that they spoke from their mouth was— "How is Shweta doing?" We have come to see her. If she is Ok or not? My mother was in shocked and she had sensed that how they came to know about it even without felling them that such drastic poison was planted in my feet? This was not just a mere coincidence. Infact this was a way to see that how bad I was feeling, or how badly I was suffering. They wanted to see my condition with their own eyes and wanted to narrate the whole episode to their dad who was the mastermind of all such negative activities. Oh! my god you people must be thinking that from where this relative appeared all of a sudden after Mr Dash!! It's my fault, in the flow of my emotions I forgot to tell you guys/gals that I was under the grip of attack. Yes, when we contacted *Guruji* later after this episode then we got to know that there was another enemy of mine, who was after my family and me, that enemy was one of my own close relatives. As I mentioned earlier that I got success at the very beginning of my life as I was good at studies and other activities, too. This was the main reason of his jealousy and hatred towards me and my family. His own children were not that much intelligent or efficient in many ways... He was not ready to digest this to see me progressing and getting countless pats on my back at all!! Hence soon after he got to know that I was out of Mr Dash and his mother's 'Black Magic' activity, he immediately trapped me in his 'Black Magic' process, so that I couldn't be able to clear IAS examination. Because he was sure about my abilities. But let me tell you guys/gals that infront of me, my family he showed us to be our best well-wisher at all times and secretly kept on trapping me and my family into this dangerous trap. Yes, in 90 per cent cases it's seen as you own close ones, who indulge in such type of 'Black Magic' activities on you as they are aware of your habits, time table, personal belongings etc but the biggest advantage for them is that they have the access to your house too!! So, beware of close relatives or near and dear ones your never know what they have in their minds!!

Anyway, since I told you in detail about my second 'Black

Magic' attack and trap, I can now continue my journey without any further problems.

What is my option now? Just surrender to the irritation and the helplessness of being trapped again? Or get up with a positive will power and fought back? This was the exact condition of my mind at that point of time... I had to make an urgent decision and implement it too. So, I decided to fight back and once again my *Guruji* came back into the picture once the second episode repeated. I went all alone this time to him, I was angry, frustrated and agitated to the core due to these series of incidences taking place in my life and wanted to get rid of them forever now. But while I was thinking all of this on the way before I could reach to him, something really dangerous I started witnessing! Yes, readers, I looked outside the car window while travelling and I started seeing slow traffic movement!! Slow Traffic? Well yes, I mean I started feeling that everything around me is slowing down! I rubbed my eyes repeatedly to get a clean view. But nothing changed!

Finally Guruji's place came, and I stepped out of the car. I had to cross the road for reaching to his house lane. I started walking ahead, but this walk was very much different than all other walks that I used to! Everything was slow, my mind and my eyes senses were slowing down. I was struggling and stuttering to cross the road through. I knew that someone was playing with me here too, someone wanted me to die with an accident this time. Yes accident! Somehow, I managed to cross the road by creating chaos in the middle of the road with my slow senseless behaviour. I still remembered that people driving on the road would have thought of me to be an idiot for sure.. I met *Guruji* and narrated him everything. Also told him about the happenings on my way, too. The moment he heard that he advised me to go back in my car and not to step out of the house at all till the time he gave me the permission. I exactly did the same. Came back to my house, told my parents about this as told by *Guruji*. I was disappointed as my preparation for IAS enamination got stuck. Thinking about all of this, it took me to a lot of self-motivating process to get back to little normal mode. And it was early night then. I still remember the time, it was 11.30 pm in the night, I came out of my room to take water from the kitchen area and my drawing room comes in the middle. While crossing the drawing room I saw a strange glimpse! I came back to re-notice it, OH MY GOD, was the statement that came out of my mouth instantly. I saw three horrifying looking women sitting on my three-seater sofa and looking inwards me quietly. I got really scared, my throat was dried and I could feel nervousness and asking for water! But then suddenly something really stranged happened this time...Yes! strange is the word. All of a sudden my fear, fright went out of the window!! And I got so much irritated and frustrated that I went near to that sofa myself looking at these horrifying faces and shouted badly "Get out of my house you evil creature" just get out, I am not scared of you at all now, and I started remembering "Goddess Kali" visualising her power and fearless strength and I was getting lots of courage by doing this. The next thing that I saw was that these evil creature started getting uncomfortable with my fearlessness and bravity and started disappearing one by one.

Within two minutes, all these evil creature were disappeaned, and there was nothing on my sofa once again. I turned back and saw my mother and brother standing behind me, looking at me with strange curiosity. They asked me. What was going on here? I told them exactly about the whole story and they could actually see the fearlessness in me. They didn't know how to react after hearing my thoughts and narration. The only thing that came out of their mouths was — "What the hell is going on in this house"? Then all of us went back to sleep.

Readers, just take a break from this narration saw or try to imagine the state of mind of that person who saw the real spooky creature and was still trying to live and want to lead normal life... Yes, it can be very disturbing !! But the key is not to give up at any point of time. And that's exactly what I did !! Now, please all of you come back to the track of active listening once again and lets continue..

So, next morning I went to *Guruji* and he promised me to protect me by giving the biggest and the strcngest form of spiritual protection of *"Goddess Kali"*. He told me to go back home and rest in peace till the next morning. I will be given a full profection. I believed him and went back. And yes I realised that till whole one week I was Ok and saw nothing, when I said nothing, I mean no evil thought, no evil creative, no illusions of accidents or mistakes. So then, my *Guruji* confirmed that everything was under control now. And yes, three months passed by, I was Ok, hence I decided to start working again. Yes, decided to come back to the corporate world of B.P.O's, but this time not the night shifts but the morning hours! Hence, decided to work as a freelance worker this time. I started contacting the different consultancy houses for this new carrier of mine!! And very soon I got an opportunity to be a freelancer for "Mothers Pride a play school, for conducting a "Teach the Teachers" programmer, where you needed to teach the teachers who were inexperienced and not efficient in their communication skills and pronunciation. I was happy in getting back working mode once again!! Soon after that workshop ended, I got another workshop of conducting a "Soft skill programme" for "American School of languages", even that I did quite successfully. Another project with "Frankfin Airhostess Academy" for communication workshop, then came the "JSS College" workshop, I had to again be a part of "Voice and Accent" programme, working on their regional accent and preparing them for campass interviews. Everything was going fine, but still deep down within me I was not happy about my achievement whenever I used to sit alone every time my past miseries, helplessness, difficulties, fear, horror used to knock at me. I could not forget my I.A.S. aspiration being spoiled and my golden years of life had been wasted due to black magic and supernatural activities. Yes, I was unable to forget this irrepairable damage and loss. Seeing death so closely made me very strong indeed, but also made me think about the cause, the seed, the root that made all of these possible! Yes, I wanted to know about this therapy, process, the way this occurs and the way it is mechanised. Because somewhere within me I felt that this process of "*Tantra*" is far more advanced than today,'s I.T. Field though it is unexplainable, where people actually seen helplesness and landed into such major problems. Problems which are not easily detectable and problems which cannot be believed by all too!!

My inquisitiveness to get into the secrets of this unknown world which destroyed my golden years started getting a new start. But the biggest of all, I want to know how the evil conduct of Black Magic imposed on the innocent people left them in a state of helplessness and even they die in this unknown process which is conducted on them. For me this work or, this effort from my side of helping other made me feel relaxed and deeply satisfied from within. So, for couple of days this fight within me was going on that whether I should go for this field or not, because it is very dangerous and life risking too. But then, I got the answer from my inner voice— "Life and death is in almighty's hand, He is the supreme saviour and protector, no one can harm you if his blessings are with you, and God always protects the innocent in his own ways". Hence, don't be scared of facing the truth anytime, just remember that your intention should be cleared that's all what matters to god!! Realising this from within, I used to feel more confident and more chanellised towards my mission of destroying each evil act done by black-magic around me. But did not know the correct way or how to start this new journey!! Because taking the first step into this would land me into "Risking-my-life" zone once again, and I was an alien in this unknown world. I was a victim of this i wanting to be a spiritral healer from a victim, which is a big gap but i wanted to get it, and thinking about this in reality, seemed a long long way to go!! Hence, I was just, in the middle of so many thoughts at one time!! Looking for a start, a way out, a healer myself.

So, finally one day, I went to my mother and shared my view point with her. Hearing me, instantly she replied back, "It is a wonderful thought and a very noble thought too, if you want to help the trapped victims of black magic. You should start thinking about it more seriously". Go to *"Maa Kali"*, sit in front of her and share your thought with her have the faith and she will surely help you. She will surely show you the correct path for this noble cause. Only *"Goddess Kali"* can help you... Getting inspiration from my mother, I got enough motivation and decided to jump into this field for helping the victims for sure now! But there is a famous saying. "Easier to say but difficult to done"!! This was just a seed which was generated in my mind. But the path was very tricky as it was full of struggles, sacrifices, will-power, self-control, immense faith, learning, acceptance, surrender, devotion and several other crucial factors which definitely come into my mind.

You readers, must be wandering that how, all of a sudden, I started thinking on spiritual line! Let me answer this to you... It takes just a moment to decide the biggest decision of life, it transforms your life-style, your thinking roots, your perception towards living your life. So that moment can arrives anytime! The challenge is to recognise it, respect it and move towards it with confidence and faith in yourself. It can simply change your life. Or should I say— "It was life changing moment for me.!" Yes it was true. Lets figure out as to how?

So, then from the next morning, I started thinking about my new path that I had choosen. So I went to the nearby temple and silently offered my prayers to God "Please help me to embrace this difficult yet spiritual path, I want to understand this spiritual power deeply and want to free from the grip of it to the victims who are being trapped in this Black Magic zone, I am seriously want to free from the grip of it to the innocent ones, help me please, help me god." Then I turned back and started moving towards my house.

And trust me my dear friends and readers after this thing there was no looking back for me. Because, soon after, I reached my house, I started worshipping *"Goddess Kali"* day and night, started fasting under my Guruji's guidance, starting chanting her *mantras*, *shlokas* and went into deep meditation practices, selfcontrol activities with complete devotion etc. From that day, my worship, my prayers, my dedication started increasing and came up to such a level that one day I just went to meet one of my friends in Gurgaon after a very long time. She was staying with another friend of her in that apartment. I was happy to see both of them. In the afternoon, my friend wanted to pick up her clothes from one of the boutique nearby only. So she told me to give her a company. I agreed. Both of us went to that boutique, it was situated in the residential area and infact was in the owner's house. The moment I entered the house my body started vibrating and this was alarming for me. We went in the room where the boutique was and there I saw a young lady sitting with her child along with her mother. The moment I looked towards her, I started speaking myself about her life, her sufferings with black magic that she was being trapped in, everything without anybody telling or narrating it to me!! She was shocked and she started crying hearing all of this. I was surprised, my friend was zapped too!! She agreed that yes which all that you have said in word is by word correct. And her mother was surprised too and started asking me that who I was and how was I able to announce such details about her daughter's life? I told her that I was a victim of 'Black magic' one year back, and after that I started worshipping *"Goddess Kali"* and now I could catch any sort of negativity instantly by the blessings of *Goddess Kali*. The moment I see any face of the victim or enter that place I could detect it. They were silently hearing this for two minutes. After that they asked me to help them!! I said that I will do whatever is possible to get you out of this 'black magic' trap for sure. This is my promise to you. But I want you to help you in condition, you have to keep complete faith in me and follow my instructions without questioning and reasoning. If you agree to this, then I am there with you to bring you out of this. Both mother and daughter agreed.

So, then we exchanged our phone number. My friend who took me to the boutiquc was stunned by hearing all of this! She had completely forgotten about her cloths and !!! She asked me that what the hell was going on there Shweta? I replied back to her saying that you just relax. I know what I am doing and just let me do what is required. You stay away from this completely. I don't want you to get into any problem. So, amicably she stepped back.

From that day that young lady's well-being was my target.

I am not disclosing her name here because of the confidentiality clause that I hold with all my victims, for their security and privacy. Hence, you will be knowing her as they "Young lady" in this book. So when I went back home I studied her case, visualising her face and all the kind of 'black magic' that was done on her came in front of me in detail. My biggest worry was her life. Because she was trapped by a "*Jinn*" a Male *jinn,* who used to rape her in the night while she was sleeping. She could feel that completely but was unable to stop it, because there was no one that she could see or touch!! Yes, my readers every night she was getting raped by this "Male *Jinn*". She even went to several *"Tantrics"* and "*Ojhas*", "*Moulavis,*" *"Pundits*". But nothing helped her at all. Infact few of them had the intention of exploiting her being she is a female. She narrated me an incident where she went to one of the "*Black Magic*" practitioner who gave her a remedy that after touching her on her breast area he would be able to feel whether that "*jinn*" was present in her body or not!! Oh my god!! Hearing this, my blood was boiling and told her that you won't surrender to such bull-shit conduct, come what may! Infact you should report against such exploitation to teach him a lesson. But she denied by saying that she doesn't have the confidence and the strength for this at this point of time. The only things she is wanting on top most priority is to get rid of this "rape" every night. Because this is disturbing her mentally till then . I understood her worry and misery being a girl myself and controlled my anger and irritation that had occurred after hearing the disgusting behaviour of so-called healers.

That day my readers, I understood one thing for sure that in this field of 'black magic', the people who call themselves as so-called *Tantric*, *Baba's*, *Ojhas* in majority are exploiters and after seeing a female victim, their intention turn into evil acts. And definitely there has to be a lady to enter this field so that women victims could approach her without getting exploited and without any fear or hesitation. My belief and my decision of entering this field became more stronger after hearing this hard, blunt truth from a woman-victim. So, before I continue further with how that "young lady" got rid of her 'black magic', I want all my female readers to take a lesson from this story that never ever surrender to any such touching demands of any male member ever no matter how much fear or urgency they create in front of you. You cannot be weak and definitely not compromise with your respect and dignity at any cost. I have even seen the most educated and well-settled women surrendering to the demands of such frauds, too. My only suggestion to all the family members and women who are reading this book is that for god's sake please apply your brain a bit, your being educated should not let you come into such traps. Yes, if you are a victim then for sure you are going through tremendous misery already but that just doesn't means that you are ready to be a second victim in this so called process of being cured by somebody, who is just trying to use you physically by creating a fear factor in your mind. Infact from now onwards the moment you hear this kind of process of cure, you should be aware that this is a strong form of fraud happening with you and you should immediately pull yourself out of this. I advice the ladies reading this that treat this problem as gynocologist problem or consulting a lady doctor. Ok, what I mean is that the way you are comfortable with a lady doctor in expressing your views and heath problems in comparison to any male doctor. Similarly, it would be far more advisable for you to contact a lady spiritual healer and a paranormal expert so that you have a better comfort level and understanding level with her. Being a lady you will not have any fear of sexual harassment issue too with her. Think about your family and your safety first. I am writing this book because I want these problems to come in front of everybody openly so that precautions can be taken regarding such activities, where this area is never spoken about. Hope, all the women who are reading this bork have got my advice and point. "Be alert and be safe".

Ok lets proceed with that incompleted story... Yes, so I told that young lady about pulling herself back from any male healer, who were having the intentions of exploiting her in the name of healing. She agreed on this and I assured her that I will surely get her out of this problem. In reply, she said, I trust you completely and would follow whatever you advice me to do. When someone starts trusting you completely then it is your responsibility towards that person increases even more. The same happened in this case too. I had great responsibility for her now.

That night I came to her house in Gurgaon and told her to sit alone in the bedroom after 11 in the night and not to speak a word after that. I was sitting outside her room, waiting for that "*jinn*" to arrive. I started my enchanting in silence from outside and the moment I feet that the "*jinn*" entered the house I also went inside the room in the darkness and told her not to say a word, and I assured her not to be scared of at all. The "*jinn*" was trying to come near her, but was unable to it and retured that night. That night was the first one when she was not sexually exploited by that "*jinn*". She slept in peace that night. The next morning I told her that she will have to come to my *Guruji* for getting an instant cure from this "*jinn*" attack. I took her along to my *Guruji* and just by seeing her, he tied a "Sacred thread" on her waist saying that now she will never be troubled by any "*Jinn*" again!! It took him just five minutes to do this. She was surprised by this gesture. After that she was out of this problem and never had the problem of "*jinns*" ever-again. I want to clarify one thing here that I was very newe in this field at that time, hence could not take the risk of experimenting the powers for curing that lady, hence took her to my *Guruji* instantly for getting immediate relief. This was my honest dealing with her.

After that permanent cure she contacted me for another problem. The problem of her mother-in-law. Yes, her marriage was on the strong edge of breaking, due to evil practice conducted by her mother-in-law. She had done a love marriage. She was a Punjabi and the guy was Jain. So their parents were not ready but finally given their consent discontenly in the end. But silently her in-laws were giving her a very tough time. Extra work load, no time with the husband, no going out for holidays or movies fight being created deliberately between husband and wife. Husband always taking side of his mother in the unreasonable demands. Even when she was pregnant her husband was least bothered. Never took care of her, the mother-in-law used to create differences between them all the time. Her health was going for a big loss, medicines were not affecting her body at all. Husband used to beat her and even said that even if you die, I don't care. Add to her wois, the mother-in-law told her to get out of the house and take care of her own expenses too while she was pregnant!! The young lady even tried to commit suicide once out of this frustration all around her. That was the time, her mother contacted me again with then new problem!! I was shocked after hearing this, because knowing in that she was pregnant and then going through such sufferings was just unacceptable.

I went to meet her. Seeing her I got so much angry that I decided to go and meet her mother-in-law and her husband. But she stopped me to do that with request. Saying that please don't go there. My mother-in-law did some kind of 'black magic' on me and my husband so that we should part our ways and she wanted to control her son completely. She told me that her hair, hanky and several other things were seen by her in her mother-in-laws cupboard once. There was and other strange looking items too. There was something that she dissolvesd in her son's food whenever she returns from her *Babaji* that she used to visit every atternate week. And whenever she returned from there, she started fighting, creating problems for her, negativity starts in the house. She was hundred per cent sure that she was practsing some kind of 'black magic' on her. This time it was for breaking her marriage with her husband.

I told her that last time also that "*Male Jinn*" was sent by your mother-in-law side only!! But I did not reveal this to her so that there should not be any fight regarding this in future. Then I told her to calm down, as I would be doing the complete case-study for her that night. I went back home. And studied her case minutely. And yes, each and everything that the young lady had narrated above regarding her mother-in-law misconduct came out to be true. Infact more hidden aspects came out in the light. I immediateley called her up and gave her the complete feedback. My instructions to her were to get out of that house urgently and start staying at her mother's place till the time the cure will take place. Because her child's life was also in danger along with *her's!* She did the same. I started my healing therapy to cure her, it took me six months to get her out of his 'black magic' done by her mother-in-law completely. Because, she was pregnant and she was trapped into this majorly hence her body had become so weak due to excessive cruelty done by the opponent that the time to cure her completely took to six months for a permanent linesafety therapy.

Today she is fine, know there is no danger to her life. She went through lot of sufferings that I couldn't even mention here. The only few major hints that I was able to share regarding her which I did. The reason is, I want everybody to learn something out of this each incidence that I am specifying and take a moral out of each story, or should I say "Case 1". Yes, this was my "Case 1" : (Women Raped By Male Jinn and Black Magic Problem)

Moral of the Story : For all the women, who are trapped in 'black magic' never agree to any sexual harassment at the name of healing from anybody. Apply your mind and never compromise on your dignity ever.

Let's Move on to My Case 2 Now : (Suicidal Case and Love Problem Case)

So, after the completion of the young lady's case, I feet really happy and satisfied with the kind of work and helping hand I had provided and this experience gave me more confidence and faith to move towards my goal more resolutely. I was completely convinced about entering and understanding this field in detail now. So, I went ahead with my spiritual growth, meditation, enchantng of *Mantras,* etc., to drown deeper into its levels. While I was doing all this "*Sadhna*" this "young lady" again contacted me!! No, not for her own problem!!

She had a friend who had recently come from Kashmir. She was working one of the leading Call Centers of Gurgoan. If I am not wrong it was "Global Vantage". She was going through depression syndrome. She had tried to cut her hand, vein several times, along with trying to jump from her house balcony too out of frustrations. She was doing all this because of her unsuccessful love with a boy. She was in love with a "cabin crew" in "Jet Airways". Both of them were young. But the boys family were not ready for their marriage, because she was a Kashmiri and he was a Punjabi. The boy suddenly backed out because of his parents wish being against his choice. He refused to marry her. Because of this she kept on calling him up again and again, he on the other had kept on rejecting her calls and proposal. In this frustration, she was trying to end her life as she had fought with her parents because of this guy and then she had come to Delhi! And in the middle only, the guy backed-off!! She had, herself visited several psychiatrist and went through different depression cure therapies before talking diffrent types of medicines, preseribad by doctors for her curing, too. But nothing was working for her at all!! She confessed to me, that yes she understand that all this was down her from dignity levels, but she just had no control on her emotions and depression. Even she wanted to get rid of this thought. But how? She didn't know....

The "Kashmiri Girl" also confessed in front of me that somewhere down in her heart she also wanted deeply, this guy to return to her. So she asked me that whether this would be possible? I told her that the guy who has backed-off in the middle is not worth-it!! Why the hell you want him back? She cried and said because— "I love him"....

Hearing this I was speechless. Seeing her helpness condition I told her that Ok I will see if he is the right guy for you then I will see, what can be done. But till that time you will promise me that you will not try to commit suicide at all ! She agreed, she will be patient enough till my case study will be done.

Separately, when I spoke to the "young lady" who got her to me, I got to know that she was about to go to some *Baba* who promised her to get her guy back with in just 48 hours!! I was shocked hearing this! The "Kashmiri Girl" was so much influenced by that *Baba* that she was ready to sell her bangles which were made of gold, given by her mother for the so-called conduct, to happen!! But somehow the

"Young lady" convinced her to wait for a while and broght her to me. Now, she wanted me to cure her wrong way of thinking and depression. She also wanted me to check whether any sort of 'black magic' was also involved in this case? I told her I would check and get back soon...

While doing the case study of the "Kashmiri Girl", I got to know that there was no 'black magic' involved in her case. But, yes, her depression syndrome was skyhigh. She had created an imbalance in her; *chakras* due to which no medicines were curing her no therapy was working on her body. Her cure was cleansing of *chakras*, removing her negative thoughts through "Vedic Healing" by *mantras* and several other meditation practices, that needed to be applied on her silently. The only way she would listen to me was, in the false hoped getting that guy back. Once she is cured, she will automatically start hating him and move on herself. It took me almost one month to cure her completely without any tablets or medical cure. She was healed with the spiritual vibrations. In the second month, she called me and said—"I don't want this good for nothing guy back in my life, he doesn't deserves me at all, thank you for showing me the right way," "I know what I need to do now with my life"... I was really happy to hear this from her!! She went to Kashmir, called me from there, her parents spoke to me, giving me blessing and thanking me for guiding their daughter correctly. They told me that from day one they knew that the guy was not loyal and worth for her... I wished them luck and felt really proud of myself as I had got one family together again!! This feeling was priceless!!

Moral of the Story: Black-magic cannot be the reason

for every problem, so don't block your mind. It can be made you imbalance of and lethargie, devoting intervally, which can be cured spiritually. Respect your life, don't waste it for anybody, suicide is done by cowards, be strong. Don't believe in *Babas'* who say we give your love back within 24 hours or 48 hours, all this is fake. Just a money-making activity.

Case study no 3 : (Property Problems, Heath Problems)

Slowly and slowly, I was moving towards my spiritual knowledge deeply. But still I was a part of this recreational world and the social circle of south Delhi. This was a purposeful choice that I made to enter into today's so-called upper society and its activities. The reason I did this was because of the stress levels, depression levels, extra-marital affair zone, infidelity, show-off, business wars, Bangkok trips, wife swapping etc was found in bulk in this zone!! Yes, its true !! I really wanted to study their life, their difficulties, their face-offs, their characteristics thoroughly. For me this was a subject. A subject that will help me to deal with real-life situations, their problems, what leads to such problems, why these people are running in search for things which are irrelevant? Why are they cheating on each other? What pleasure are they looking for? And then are they happy and satisfied after this? Hence, many such thoughts were dwelling in my mind. So my decision was to enter this zone, pretending to be one of them and being one of them will only give me the opportunity to look and understand each others' problems very closely!! Yes, my reader this was my 'Secret Operation', if you may want to call it!! So, I was mingling with many of such couples. Couples who would be on Orkut (Networking

Site) with their every small activity and not to forget every Bangkok trips too! Their faces wore fake smile but the hearts were unhappy. They wanted to show that they are the best couples, but internally they knew that nothing was going right in their relationship aspect. Fake smile, fakeness became the part of their life. But the strange part was that they would never admit! Society, social status to be maintained.... Anyways in this process I met a couple who were married for 14 years, had two children, one boy, one girl. There children were studying in D.P.S. Mathura Road. They were living in South Extension. We usually met occasionaly. There was party going-on an in-house party. The "middle-aged married women" was sitting on the couch quietly. There were several other women attending the party too. All of them were married, except me!! But my attention was going on her after every minutes, not that she was really attractive or something, but due to her negativity. I could see a black cloud like structure covering her from behind from head to toe! Yes, and it was capturing her completely. There was certainly majorly wrong with her life and her health I knew, after seeing this. But then since I had kept my profile (spiritual profile) extremely secret, I could not be loud about it in public. Hence, in a very subtle manner, I asked her separately— "Excuse me I want to tell you something If you don't mind"! She replied sure— "I told her that I can figure out negativities, and I have seen that your life is going towards negative track, so if you would feel comfortable then, you must meet me separately some day to discuss this, because you need help"!

She was surprised hearing this from me! She said that yes I would surely want to meet you to tell how I feel... Mutually we met after three days. She came along with her husband. I told her to come alone in the room with me for detail and opened discussion without her husband. So that she could talk more openly if required. She was happy with this! So then I told her that there is something majorly negative with her. Before I figure that out, is there something that she wants to tell me? Does she feel normal? Or even knows that something abnormal is happening around her? The moment I completed my question, this "middle-aged women" started her first statement saying that — "Yes, I feel something is abnormal with me! My health is not good. I think my mother-in-law and my sister-in-law are conducting evil practices, on me and my husband. To control my husband to create differences between us, my mother-in-law interferes in our life a lot. I don't know how I am surviving all these years, my children's health is also not in good shape. I am keen to have the property share so that we can do some educational and future planing for the betterment of our children. Even my husband in his business can improve if we get our property share. But whenever I try this it falls apart. Please help me if you can.. I was surprised, that she had so much to say"!!

But I assured her that relax! Just calm down. First of all your health needs to be taken into consideration because you as a woman is very important for me. Only if you are Ok, your family will be Ok in future. You have to be strong and just follow my instructions, without asking any questions. Only if you would agree to listen to me, then I will be ready to help you. She instantly agreed. She said please help me, I will follow all your instructions blindly. So I started my process by asking her children's name, her mother-in-law's name, sister-in-law's name, etc. She told me to keep this secret in front of her husband as he will not admit things regarding his mother and will lead to clashes between them. I agreed. I told her that I will do a remedy for her and her family, protect her health, her children health, property matter to be sorted for her children future. I started my work after couple of days I told her that I will have to visit your residence for remaining process to be completed. So, I reached there and went to her room where the house temple was placed. Completed my process and purification, met her children, her daughter was my favourite, very bright girl, humble, pretty and my little friend. God bless her always!! I told her that things will now start falling into the correct places for you, but just remember to be fair and humble in every step of your life after this. She became my friend. Slowly her things started improving, her health, her chidlren's health, she got the property share, got new car, went for a vocation with children. Everything became like a dream for her.

I knew through my spiritual vibrations that all this has happened due to blessings of Goddess *Maa Kali* process that I had implanted on her and on her whole family, but she never thanked me for it!! Yes its true. I was waiting and watching that when will she remember to least acknowledge my efforts. I never wanted the credit for it but wanted a humble thank you for sure. Infact this time I was back-stabbed by her in many ways in my personal life as she was my friend, and she took immense advantage of my trust and honesty that I had for her. I got to know that she and her husband used to backbite me in my absence too. Basically, they turned out to be the most thankless and the most cunning people in my journey. This time it was a lesson for me to be learnt that before you go ahead with doing something good for somebody, ideally check before whether they are worth your efforts or later on after their cure they will change colours like a chamelion and started spreading slanderous campaign against you. Because these guys misused my efforts and spiritual help that was provided to them. So this was a mistake from my side, too. And I never repeat my mistake. From this episode I took a pledge of not helping anybody without checking this after-effects of cure and also will not believe in any ones dramatic story like that quickly. I will do my investigations spiritually before saying 'yes' to anybody in future. It also taught me a lesson of not doing anything for anyone for free because people only respect your efforts and your skill whenever they have applied some of their own bit into it, they take you wore seriously once you respect your own time, energy, skills and yourself too.

Moral of the Story: Fake smiles on any networking sites can be spotted as there is a huge fake life behind! Beware of it! Beware of such thankless people who forget your contribution and your emotions and won, mind to back-stabb you. So all the spiritual healers, don't forget to check the aura and the characteristics of the victim and his after-effects. This suggestion is for all the new spiritual healers who have just made thair entry in this field!!

So, here I was very much disappointed and got hurt after this last case of mine and I decided to give myself a break from this charitable help that I was doing for a while!! Yes, I was really irritated! I just concentrated in my spiritual uplift guidance for the betterment, meditations, knowledge collection etc. Suddenly, I came across a Muslim spiritual healer who helped me in my personal zone regarding something personal that cannot be revealed here, as it was something concerning spiritual guidance for the betterment... He encouraged me to take this practice as professionally and asked the to come out in public openly. He made me understand the importance of me coming out professionally in the field globally, too. And he suggested that treat this as your profession; you need to charge for your efforts as this will be your only occupation which will give you a wider scope to reach to the victims. I was first hesitant about this pattern as this work demands lot of risk, time, energy, above all sacrifices from your personal life, too. You have to enter the world of simplicity, leave all social recreations etc. But then I kept on thinking about this for few days and then finally decided to enter this field taking this as a profession. For this, I was thinking of a respectable medium and wanted to capture the problem of 'black magic' globally. I wanted to reach to the masses globally, wanted to clear the misconception about of "*Goddess Kali*" through my honesty and devotion !

So; finally, I got my answer!! The answer was creating my own website. Yes, a website which has an "Awareness Programme" about "*Tantra*" and its meaning, clarifying its myths, educating the normal masses about different form of 'Black Magic' etc. A place where globally people could contact me, write to me with their problems, lady victims could feel comfortable with this service, explain about different paranormal activities and provide them with genuine solutions. So, I started my work towards my website and its content writing myself. Every bit that has been mentioned in my website is written by me. My idea was to use communicating form of English writting so that the language could be easily understood by the general masses also who are not very good in English too... So then the website was created by my same friend whom I had mentioned in the starting of my book, if you remember!! So then the website was ready during the "*Navaratras*" (Nine days of Goddess Durga"), by the name of www.maakalishwetasarojinimahakali.com and "www.mahakalivedichealingshelter.com". You people can check this website for getting detailed theory on each topic of Black Magic, if you are keen to know about the unknown world. It will be very informative for you! From here began my professional paid service zone, where I was available 24x7 for my victims and wanted to give a complete assurance of good results. Days kept on passing by... Victims from overseas started contacting me affected by the dangerous impact of several types of Black Magic problems. I kept on healing them one by one through their photographs. My experience was increasing, my learnings were increasing, my responsibility was increasing, my meditation was increasing. Complicated cases started dropping in all around the world slowly!! I became extremely busy. The website started getting recognition by different *Acharayas*, who personally contacted me through "Linkden" (Business Networking Site), encouraged my work, after reading it. Told me to keep up the good work. Suddenly, I started getting victims from "Fear files" a show which comes on "Zee TV". The victims started seeing my site and started contacting me by calling me on my website number and live chat too! Now, the complicated cases, several years old cases started coming to me. Let me share few complicated cases with you people from here now.

Case Study No 4 : (Maran Matra, Life Attack, Health Problem)

This case belongs to a lady staying in Mumbai. She was a chemistry teacher by profession, teaching in a famous school of Mumbai. One day in the afternoonl I got a call from her saying that she and her son are badly trapped in the grip of 'black magic' and no healer or spiritual helps reaches to them, everyone backs out and avoids them after seeing their case! Everyone assures them that they will come for their rescue but they failed to give them relief! She was very much tensed about her health and her son's health too. Her son was studying in twelvth class. Her husband was staying out of India in one of the Gulf countries, but was not caring towards her and her son! She asked for my help. I told her my protocol of case study and explained her that I cure people through their photos, so she needs to send in her photo and her son's photo in my G-mail account given in the website. She agreed and did the same. When I studied her case I was really shocked. This lady was almost on the death bed. She was trapped in by "*Maran Mantra*"— which means "a way to kill your enemy"! She was trapped into it for almost ten years. This was eating her like a slow poison. Now, her body was eaten badly like a termite eats the wood in a telling manner.

But my biggest worry was that now her body would be soon attacked by an evil soul of a lady, to enter her body and troubled her completely and finished her with no time! Yes it was true... Several other things were planted in the house where she and her son were staying, which could not be hidden by my eyes at all. But the problem was that she had reached to me very late. In the meantime, major damage had been done on her already and at that point of time she was a half-dead body for me. Skeleton is the word. Extremely weak, pale, no life in her body. She is more worried for her son than herself in this condition also. Many *Tantrics* and *Ojha's* had made her spent a lot of money before and the result was just zero!! Her husband and her relatives were behind this 'black magic' act, that was detected in the case study. I told her that I cannot keep you in the dark. So be ready to hear the truth from me.

Firstly, your case is extremely negative because you have come to me in the last stage of your disease (Black Magic), the only thing I can do is to give my best and try to save you completely, along with your son. But for this you need to trust me and follow my instructions blindly. She agreed like majority of victims. I also told her that she will have to remain completely silent till the time I will be curing her. Because talking about this can give hints to the opponent about the process of curing that she is trying to give for! She religiously followed my instructions. It took me thirty days for curing her, cleansing her body and protecting her body and her son's body. By the grace of *"Goddess Kali"* she and her son are protected today and are living a very safe and healthy life. Her health got alsight in one month only, her energy levels became normal, her face glow came back. After all this went in her favour, I asked her a question— Why did you not approach any good genuine healer before only? She replied— "Mam, in Mumbai there is no genuine spiritual healer available, they are all fake and give false promises, you should open up your franchise in Mumbai. So that people can get help from you in a genuine manner!! I was really touched by her gesture and said that I wish I become that much capable soon that I am able to set up franchise in different cities, but for now I am available through my website contact anytime! She really thanked me for my help and promised to give "Goddess Kali" all the love and respect in her house temple.

Moral of the Story: Never avoid any symptom of your health going down. Contact the doctor for help but if nothing works there, reports are normal but still your health is decreasing then don't waste time. Contact a genuine spiritual healer or a Paranormal Expert urgently. Precautions is better than cure.

Case Study No 5 : (Pregnant Woman Black Magic)

Let me share one of the most emotional cases with you people now. This case is about a pregnant lady staying in Canada. She contacted me through my website: www.maakalishwetasarojinimahakali.com and www.mahakalivedicnealingshelter.com, she wrote me a detailed E-mail regarding her problem. Her age was 28, she was a working woman, who got married in Canada with her childhood sweet-heart. This was her first-time pregnancy experience. She was in six-month pregnancy stage when she approached me. She told me that from the three months of her pregnancy she noticed few abnormal behaviour, or should I say activities. She felt that somebody was touching her womb. But the moment she puts her hand there that feeling disappeared! Then she had started getting the feeling of eating raw mutton! But she was continuously trying to avoid this desire. But every night she used to become restless for this strange habit! Sounds scary isn't it! From the fifth month onwards, she started getting a feeling of pushing her own womb with her own hands atleast once in a day! But she knew that something was forcing her to do such thing. She was very hesitant in disclosing anything regarding this to her husband as she knew he would never believe this!

Then came the six-month when she started feeling that someone is trying to press her womb with force and is scratching her womb with nails! This was very scary for her. She contacted few healers in Canada silently without telling her husband about it, but nothing really helped her. She was tensed and disturbed, due to which her stress levels were increasing and her health was not keeping too well also! Now, she wanted my help. I told her to get her case study done by sending the photo on gmail account urgently. She did so. When I sat for my case study, I was taken a back! This "Canada lady" was going through a very dangerous form of 'black-magic', in which the attack was on her life and her kid's life! Through a dangerous form of 'black magic' someone was trying to destroy her complete uterus, child, and infact make sure that she should die in this delivery process of premature baby. Yes, it was planned, that the seventh month or the eighth month, her attack would be increased to such a high degree that they will have to go for a premature delivery. And while this medical process very cleverly her life will be at risk or should I say she will be died and it would seem like a normal pregnancy complication and no one would doubt this plotting which was designed against her!! And, Oh my god, this was the sixth month when she reached to me! I was really worried to think about this case because here I had to deal with two lives together. One life which has not even entered this world! I immediately called her up directly and told her everything. I motivated her to be strong, and not get weak at all. She had to help me and her child also by not being, scared, because now she entered "*Maa Kali's* shelter". She was a very bold and strong woman, I must say. She assured me that for saving her child, she would do anything to fight back. But she just asked me one question—Who is behind all this mam? I told her, I don't disclose names of people as per the legal aspects and security purposes. But for you this time I will tell you the person behind this, only once you are safe. She agreed.

So, my curing process started, it took me twenty-one days for the situation to get into my own control. And hence protected her and her child completely. The evil practice was destroyed by "*Maa Kali's* blessings". She had a normal delivery. Had a baby boy. She was very happy. She called me from the hospital only to give me this news! I gave her blessings and wished her good luck. After a weeks time, she again called me to ask me that who was the culprit mam, you promised me that you would tell me after things get back to normal! I took a deep breath and said— It was your own husband dear... He is having an extra-marital affair and he wanted to finish you and your child without any legal hassles, hence he opted for this 'black-magic' process. Now, I leave it on you to decide what you need to do! She disconnected the line after hearing this. A month later again she called me informing me that she has filed for divorce and has moved out of that house to her parents house. She has decided to work again. It came as a surprise to me that she was a "lawyer" herself! Today she is doing fine with her son and parents.

Moral of the Story: In 'Black Magic' anything is possible. You cannot trust the closest relation also. Infact people who are closest to you are responsible for this, as they know your weakness and have an easy access to your life.

Case Study No. 6 : (Black Magic Practise of South Africa, Life Attack)

This case was equivalent to five cases in one!! Yes, my readers, how? You will understand once you read through! My website: www.mahakalivedichealingshelter.com and www.mahakalishwetasarojinimahakali.com had letter for me! The letter came from a man from New Zealand. He was divorced, age more than 43 years and father of three children who were teenagers staying in South Africa. The wife had completely ignored him all of a sudden. He was alone and was writing to me after saving his life once from a major life attack from 'black magic' done to him from South Africa! There was a spiritual healer, who was an old lady and a true devotee of Goddess *Maa Kali*, who had saved his life that time but now she was no more... And after five years again he had been experiencing the same kind of misery all of a sudden. This time this victim actually knew quite a bit about what was wrong with him because of that genuine old lady who actually helped him before!! But still I told him to send his photo for the case study, because nothing can be remained hidden after the case study! He followed the protocol. I started his case study. The result came out to be very inhuman. This "New Zealand Man", was suffering from a South African local 'Black Magic' practice where they used a dead body or should I say a soul after death which flies all over around the victim's body and surrounding and was very difficult to capture. This is there to end the victims prosperity and in the end take him toward miserable death. Miserable death because it causes major diseases in victims, body and put him in lot of pains and suffering. But in this case, there was not one dead body used to finish him off but also, there were five dead bodies used against this "New Zealand Man"! It means five spirits with evil practices were used against him. But he was under the impression that only one dead body was used against him for destruction. He was continuously getting dreams in which he was seeing himself trapped in 'black magic' process with different things used in 'black magic', sometimes the attack was on his neck, sometimes the attack was on his head and mainly the attack was done in his eyes for making him blind!!

This 'black magic' process was done on him for the second time from South Africa where his enemies, relatives who were practicing this act were staying. It was a couple. They were completely jeolous of his growth at his early years and even his good relation with his wife. Hence, they wanted to destroy his happiness, prosperity, health, relation, social statue to make his life miserable. But there conduct came in lime-light also before because of a spiritual healer— (the old lady worshipping *"Maa Kali"*, she saved him from it. But after her death they planted it again with an evil intention. And this time it increased from one dead body to five dead bodies negativity on this man!! He was going through debts. But still they wanted him to suffer more! Because a legal property was waiting for him, if he was cured completely. He arranged for the finances for this remedy urgently because he was going through a hard time. Whatever he could arrange, I agreed to accept it and put my share into it too, as this was a challenging case for me too. And above all I could not see someone would die due to 'black-magic' practice. The curing process took me thirty days in whole, but everything came into control. He was doing Ok now, and he wrote me a long E-mail about expressing his thoughts after he was getting cured. Thanking me and *"Maa Kali"* for protecting him. Now, he again contacted me over his money matter, property matter. But that is not very difficult case that needs to be mentioned here. Thank you *"Maa Kali"* for guiding me this challenging case and turning it into a success. *Jai Maa Kali...*

Moral of the Story: Some people have misconception that overseas countries do not have Black Magic problems. Only India is a superstitious country! But my dear readers I get more victims from overseas than India!! Black Magic has its roots around the world!!

Case Study No. 7 : (Wodoo Doll, Putla Tantra, Marriage Destruction)

Now, this one takes me way back to those days when I was a victim of this. Yes, I mentioned in the starting about a group of people connected to "Mr Dash" who refused to believe me when I used to tell them about my supernatural feeling! They thought I was talking senseless thing! My helplessness was not understood by them at all... Anyway, let me come back to the case now!! So one day at 12.30 in the night I got a SMS on my cell from the guy. This guy was common friend between me and "Mr Dash" in the past! He was also my junior from DPS Noida. Now, he was working with "EXL Service, Noida center" in a "Middle Management Position" in one of the international process. I had his number saved in my cell. The SMS said: Hello, Shweta sorry to disturb you so late in the night, but my wife is going through strange abnormal activities, I am scared and worried for her. Please can you help? Thanks. And there were two missed calls too! Unfortunately, that night my cell was somehow on silent mode, hence I could not read the SMS on time! The next morning, when I checked my cell, I read this SMS, and immediately I called him back. I explained him about the delay. And asked him what really happened? He stated—Shweta my wife is getting "Black cross marks" all over her body, they appear automatically on her body and then fade away with leaving a red mark sometime. She is fainting, shouting and behaving quite weirdly these days. These marks are spreading all over her body. She is getting horrifying dreams of big bones, skeletons, she is being inside a circle which is outlined with big white bones without any flesh on them! Her body is paining and she is very much frightened by this. Even I am really worried. I remember you used to talk about similar supernatural activity troubling you, hence thought that may be you could put some light into this matter! He knew about my website: www.maakalishwetasarojinimahakali.com and www.mahakalivedichealingshelter.com through facebook, knew that I because a spiritual healer and a paranormal expert now. I told him that I would want to proceed with the case study and he should send me the photo of his wife immediately on my Gmail account: (shwetasarojinimahakali@gmail.com).

He instantly did that. When I did her case study, then I got to know that the 'black magic' was not only done on his wife who was working in "Accenture Noida" but was on him too. On his wife these "Black Marks" being formed automatically were due to a process that is based in 'black magic' in which your whole body is being trapped by putting markings all over. Actually these marks were put on her "*Putla*" or "Doll" that was made on her name! Yes, that "*Pulta*" or "Doll" was considered to be her body in Black Magic process, where she could be completely operated through that "*Putla* or Doll". Her health was in real danger. And the guy was trapped in a way where he could be extremely reactive and his carrier path was blocked and his marriage and relationship with his also disturbed by that he could not live a normal a married life, and be divorced his wife. Even the girl was trapped in such a way that she whould loose attraction for him and think of separating from him at a fast pace. All this was done from by relative only, who belonged to their village. I did not disclosed the name of that person as per the legal policy and security of our company. Moreover, never wanted them to blame each other families during any arguments.

I just told then about the actual problem and the process of curing for it. It suggested him and his wife to contact someone from their family reference for cure. But they told me that there is no one that they knew. Nor their families will believe in this, because they have never faced this kind of supernatural activities. Hence, both of them told me to take charge of their cases and solve it permanently. I agreed, but reminded the guy about how none of them believed me when I was in pain!! He was bit embarrassed about the whole past. But my idea was not to demean him or make him feel guilty. My point was to make sure that he doesn't repeat this mistake with his wife this time at any cost.

So then the process of curing started. It was a complicated case. "*Putla* or the doll" needed to be destroyed before doing anything! Damages made in her body needed to be healed and cleansed. Everything together took me thirty-six days in total for creating a permanent protection for both of them. So, today they are fine and happy together. They thanked me after the cure. Somewhere down the line, I also left that may be now he would feel and understand that how tough it would have been for me when I was going through those helpless phase all alone!!

Moral of the Story: Never ignore or overlooked the supernatural existence ever, you never know when it gives a knock at your door too...

Case Study No. 8 : (Black Magic case of 2 years old Baby Boy)

This case is of a two years old baby boy! Yes, only two years old, you heard right!! The promotion of my website:www.mahakalivedichealingshelter.com and www.mahakalishwetasarojinimahakali.com started in a local medium also. That medium was in paper ad. So after one week of promotion I got a call from a mother. A "young mother" with a two years old baby boy. She introduced herself and then hesitantly asked me about if I could help her in a strange matter of her child. She narrated that her child is just two years old and is extremely violent and furious with people and his age group children too! He beats them, hits them, and runs suddenly towards the road side full of traffic. It was very much embarrassing for her as a mother when people came with complains and she had to face the music later! She was really worried for him. She and her husband also went to the counsellor for advice but in return the counsellor blamed her for certain things and advised to do something which she tried but not yielded desired results. Now, since she was available in the house 24 hours for the child, as usual people would blame her for such conduct of the child! Her husband was generally travelling for work. I told her to visit my website and read "Protection of new-born child" page in detail before anything else. This would give her a fair idea about where this situation is hinting! She did that and called me back for getting the case study done. I proceeded. The case study showed me the result. The baby's hair was taken during his "ceremony of *mundan*" (hair cutting ceremony of child) by a lady of their family, who has a personal grudge with this mother and never wanted to see her happy due to jealousy factor. So, instead of directly hampering her, she took a way of harming her kid. As for every mother her child is her biggest weakness. She wanted to see her sulking, seeing her child's accident taking place, the child in future would be operated in such a manner where he would start harming himself too. His health would go for a toss. Both of them would be running to hospitals very soon. This was the plan of action. As it is the planets of that kid were very much on the aggressive side, and this was gazed by the opponent by knowing the exact *kundali* timing and date of birth of the child! Hence, such form of 'black magic' was opted which would take him more towards aggression, so that it could make an inpact on baby's behavioural issue.

I told the vicitim's mother about everything that I diagnosed from the case study. She was irritated by that woman and agreed about hair being taken, and agreed that from that time only change in the child had started. She told me to proceed with the cure on urgent basis for the protection of her child. She arranged the finances all by herself. She knew that her husband would never agree on this! But she knew what was happening! I started the cure. It took me twenty-five days for the whole protection to be made for the "New-born child". Today he is safe, and his aggression is still there but his life is back to normal and above all no 'black magic' will aftect his life due to the grace of "*Maa Kali's* protection". *Jai Maa Kali...*

Moral of the Story: Sometimes women have to take independent decision, before it gets too late. Be alert, so that nobody could take away your baby's hair and nails for conducting Black Magic. Get your "New-born baby" protected before it's too late. Precaution is better than cure. Because in the "*Kalyug* times", no one can see your happiness. So many couples are without children and they cannot see someone else enjoying that happiness!

Case Study No 9 : (Love Problem by Black Magic)

This case came to me from Dubai. A 25-years-old girl wrote to me on my Gmail account after reading my website: www.mahakalivedichealingshelter.com page of "Marital problem" section. This page talks about different types of marriage problems and its remedies. She was unmarried. She contacted me for a before marriage problem! Yes, she got engaged with a guy in Dubai itself. This was a love-turned family acceptance relation. But suddenly the boy backed out and backed off from the engagement! This "Dubai girl" was depressed and wanted to understand the reason behind this, and wanted the guy back in her life too! So, I told her that I will find out the reason through the case study and soon update her on this. So, then I studied her case. And the result came out to be like this: The girls parents agreed for the marriage but one of the relatives was not happy to see the girl getting a good groom, who is economically sound. Hence, she did this 'black magic' on the guy, by controlling his mind and diverting the attraction towards the "Dubai girl". Now, the guy didn't wanted to see her face or talk to her even! On the other hand, her relative out of jealousy blocked her marriage with evil practices, so that she could not be able to get married in future also. When I did the case study for that guy the results were not very positive, too. The guy's character was not very clear, meaning the guy would be always interested in other women as well and will mentally torture her later after marriage. So, I was not in the favour of this marriage after this detection. I told her everything. I said that it proved to be a "blessing in disguise" because you wouldn't be happy with this guy. He will not changed after marriage! I will not advice you to be with him any more. Rest is your desire! What I can do for you is, open the marriage blockage which had been created by 'black magic' and you would soon start getting good well-settled marriage proposals. Think about it. She instantly replied that I always had doubts about my boy friend, but without having any proof against him and my feelings for him used to make me meet away every time but after hearing from you about his character, I am sure that I was right. Please help me in forgetting him and remove my marriage blockage so that I could get the right person for myself. Also protect me from such evil acts for lifetime mam. I assured her that this will be done in thrity days. She followed my instructions thoroughly and after three months she got married in London with a well-settled guy. She had sent me the photographs of marriage and thanked me for my help by calling me later. I really felt happy for her. God bless you my dear. *Jai Maa Kali*...

Moral of the Story: Sometimes people are not the way they look or present themselves. Don't be blind in love, at least be sure that the person for whom you are trusting so much, is that person worth for that trust or not. Be strong

enough to kick that person out of your life. Never approach any *baba*, *Tantric* for *vashikaran* practics, it will never give you natural love and its beauty.

Case Study No. 10 : (Black Magic to destroy Woman's Beauty)

This case will be really shocking for all the female readers! How? Read on... A girl from Australia wrote me an e-mail saying that I want to look beautiful again, can you help me *Guru Mata*? I am 28 years old, unmarried girl. I was really beautiful two years back. But now I look ugly. There is definitely something majorly wrong with me in a supernatural way *"Guru Mata"*, please save me, I am really fed up with this look of mine. I have tried all kinds of skin treatments but nothing has worked for me at all. My face, skin is turning from bad to worse. She herself had sent me her photo for case study along with the consultation fee, specified in the website! She had also sent me her earlier copies of photo and then two years later after-effect photo too. I was shocked myself! This could not be true!! For few seconds I was numb. I couldn't sleep that night, and couldn't concentrate in other cases for that night! I was eager to study the case for this problem this time and wanted to know the reason. But I had to wait for the complete *"Puja samagri"* to reach to me (products needed for case study). Next day till the afternoon I got the stuff ready with me. I immediately sat down for the case study. What I saw was disgusting.... This girl was actually suffering from a very high level and a high degree of 'black magic' process. This process was used in ancient times by secretive *Tantrics* only. This is a very powerful process by which you can take away someone's beauty, age and pass it on to others who is looking for getting pretty. Meaning in simple words, exchanging beauty with ugliness! Yes, it is true. But this process is rarely implemented because, not many *Tantrics* are aware of its complete implementation. But this was used this time on this girl. This time it was not done by any family member or relatives, etc. But she had eaten a fruit which she purchased from the super market herself. It was a pear. Yes, it was kept very smartly in the fruits section so that anyone who would pick this up and eat it will get the communicable 'black magic' process on her. This was designed for a female member only. Yes, it is true, and it is very much possible. Within one month her beauty, glow started fading away, and the female for whom this process was implemented would have started gaining her beauty and she was passing her beauty problems to her! Her hair fall started, her skin rashes started, wrinkles started, skin started changing complexion towards the dark side, under-eye marks. Basically, she was not the same person that she was before due to this 'black magic'. And in two years she had made enough damage on herself. I immediately called her up and briefed her about the problem. She was started crying badly. I consoled her and told her to be strong. There is a solution for this but it is lengthy and demands heavy fees as well as patience. By the god's grace she belonged to a very rich family, the only thing that was challenging for her on the patience aspect. But she assured me that she will do whatever it takes for getting her beauty back. I told her that this would take at least six months for me to cure the evil effects and protect you completely from it. Then six months your beauty get back slowly towards you. Only if you can be patient for twelve months with me and trust me completely, I would take up this case. She said she will do whatever I tell her to do from this very moment and requested me to take her case on priority basis. I also understood her pain and agreed. It was a complete team work. She was very cooperative and sensible girl. We started slowly and completed first six months. She was completely blocked from accepting any further communicable disease. Then came the next six months. Here, we made different spiritual beauty products for her, which were specially energised by me for eleven days each and that was sent to her for applying on her face. All this hardwork and patience went into this process of curing her. It did not take six months for her to be cured but took only four months for her to regain her beauty. Her hair took some more time for cure. But then she got back her beauty this time! Because of the spiritually energised products. These produce are mentined in our website : mahakalivedichealingshelter.com. Anybody can read the details there. Many women have been benefited by then. She found this to be a miracle! Her family member really thanked me a lot and promised me that whenever they will visit India, they would definitely want to meet me in person. I felt satisfied after healing this girl, I got her smile back, with the grace of *Maa Kali*. Thank you *Maa Kali*...

Moral of the Story : Be very careful with your beauty, be very alert in eating, don't trust any person, don't talk big about your beauty, keep a low profile, and get yourself protected if you are really beautiful. Because 'Black Magic' can snatch away it something that is priceless from you too!!

So, as I said before that I have long series of cases week me available. These ten cases were just a trailer among the worst of them!! Yes, its true, I will have to write another book on these cases for sure. Because they are too many of them. These cases were just presented to you as examples, so that you readers could get a fair idea of different kinds of cases which come to us regurding Black Magic Sufferrings on regular bases. For more you can also go through the regular updated "Testimonial section" in the website, where the victims have mentioned their problems and solutions too!! We also have a section of victims audio in our website : www.mahakalivedichealingshelter.com where few victim have recorded their voice and spoken about their Black Magic Journey. I do recommend my readers too listen to these audios, atleast for once. This will enlighten you more about to this unknown world's power and its consequences.

Now a days, I get atleast 40-50 calls per day asking for help from 'black magic' sufferings from India and overseas. Plenty of *E-mails* from people around the world looking for a genuine spiritual help and solution. Each case that I take become a learning experience for me, each case has its own challenge and difficulties attached to it. But I know only one thing that no evil can be more powerfull than sacred spiritual power. The only challenge is to reach to the correct genuine place where truly your problems would be solved and moreover heard and felt.

Today by the grace and blessings of "*Maa Kali*" I could able to form my own Private Ltd Company in the name of : **"MAHA KALI VEDIC HEALING SHELTER PVT. LTD"** in which I am the president and my mother Sarojini is the director. This company deals with several spiritual aspects. We provide genuine case study feedback to our victims within 3-4 days of their booking with us. We give them the flexibility of getting the case solved by any of their own spiritual healers after the case has been detected too and the real problem has been diagnosed. Because sometimes the cure doesn't takes place due to lack of detection programme. The company also guides the people who are sometimes just misguided by several *Tantrics* and so-called spiritual healers, who create fear factor in their minds to make money out of them, even when there is no Black Magic on them We clearly tell them after the case study that its just their psychological block that they feel that its 'black magic' that they are suffering from, whereas there is nothing like that in reality, so that they should not be trapped in any fraud.

The mission of **"MAHA KALI VEDIC HEALING SHELTER PVT. LTD."** is to help the victims trapped in Black Magic and several other Astrological problems by giving them correct solution without misguiding them. Making sure that *"Goddess Kali's"* image should not be exploited any further for any mean *tantric* practises. People should start keeping place to Goddess *Kali's* photo in their house temples without any fear. She is a loving and compassionate goddess who always protects her devotees from evil forces. We want to build *"Maha Kali"* temple and Ashram with her blessings in near future where several victims can come and visit her for getting power and courage from her to be used in the correct manner. This Ashram will give shelter to the helpless women who are victims of Black Magic and are troubled by their own family members for accomodation too. They can stay here till their cure is happening very silently. Donations and help is required from all parts of the world, for this dream to come true. And of course "*Maa Kali's*" blessings are required than anything else. So people who have faith in "*Goddess Kali*" can contact our company for sending donations and help for this "sacred mission".

The most important point that we want to mention here is for all the women victims. "**MAHA KALI VEDIC HEALING SHELTER PVT. LTD.**" makes sure that no sexual harassment or discomfort is caused to any women victim from our team. Women victims can they can write to me directly on my gmail account : (shwetasarojinimahakali@gmail.com). Hence, women victim please feel free to contact us without any fear.

Our company also has the provisions of conducting "*Private Yagnas*" for overseas customers, and then the, needfull accessories are send to them through couriers and postal services. "*Chandi-path*", *Saraswati ji's puja, Lakshmiji's puja, Kuberji's puja, Mahamritunjya jap, Rahu healing jap, Bagla Mukhi puja, Maa kamala puja, Maa Chinnamasta puja, Maa Bhuvneshwari puja* are also performed by us for overseas customers as well as Indian clients.

For Real Estate People, builder we have a land detection programme where we detect your land, prosperity and guide you regarding its profit-making ability. We also inform the builders about any negativity present in that land. We also have the provision of removing negativity from that land. So builders and construction people also contact us for our service.

Lot of patients who are in depression can contact us for spiritual remedies regarding their mental and stress level problems. We give cure to such victims also. And our success has been increasing gradually in this area too.

Prosperity, *puja* are another very popular segments in our website. Here any businessmen can contact us for getting the business growth and having prosperity throughout the year. They are getting good results by the grace and blessing of *Maa Kali*.

"MAHA KALI VEDIC HEALING SHELTER PVT. LTD." also has its own products available on our website: www.mahakalivedichealingshelter.com. They are all spiritual products, which are highly beneficial for trapped victims. You can refer to the website for more details. These products are sent to our overseas customers often on their request. These products are also in demand among the Indian customers too.

"MAHA KALI VEDIC HEALING SHELTER PVT. LTD" also deals with "Spiritual beauty therapy", where we make a complete package for the client. This include "antiaging spiritual cure", "spiritual body toning package" as per the body structure and body metabolism rate. "Spiritual skin glow", "Spiritual hair treatment" etc. We also provide complete "Spiritual Pre-bridal makeup" to our overseas brides, in which they get spiritual help in achieving their glow, complexion and beauty. But this facility is done only for selective clients who have the spending capacity. As it is a very ancient form and also a rare form, hence, not many can afford it. But few selective people in India and overseas have utilised this help form us and they have become our regular clients now. People interested in this process can contact me on mail : shwetasarojinimahakali@gmail.com.

We also deal with pet protection and vehicle protection, this may sound weird to you people but trust me once you will read through about these facilities you will understand its importance. Do read the page: "Pet-protection and vehicle protection" in our, website which has a new name now : www.mahakalivedichealingshelter.com. If you have a pet and you are a "Pet-lover" then you should not miss this section!

Today many students from North Campus, New Delhi contact me for curiosity reason regarding paranormal activities, they want to learn this and understand this. Infact, "Shri Ram College of Commerce, New Delhi" student took my interview for their college project based on Paranormal Activities. They contacted me from google being a "Paranormal expert". My live interview is present on YouTube by the name of "Shweta Bisht paranormal expert". All readers can hear me out there, if they like. So today I am completely devoted to *Maha Kali's* spiritual healing methods and my only mission is to remove *Maa Kali's* fear from every